10 Ways to Build Your World Vision

A MIND FOR MISSIONS

Paul Borthwick

NAVPRESS

A MINISTRY OF THE NAVIGATORS
P.O. BOX 35001, COLORADO SPRINGS, COLORADO 80935

The Navigators is an international Christian organization. Jesus Christ gave His followers the Great Commission to go and make disciples (Matthew 28:19). The aim of The Navigators is to help fulfill that commission by multiplying laborers for Christ in every nation.

NavPress is the publishing ministry of The Navigators. NavPress publications are tools to help Christians grow. Although publications alone cannot make disciples or change lives, they can help believers learn biblical discipleship, and apply what they learn to their lives and ministries.

Library of Congress Catalog Card Number: 87-62360
ISBN 08910-91912

Cover photograph: Martin Crabb

Scripture quotations in this publication are from the *Holy Bible: New International Version* (NIV), copyright © 1973, 1978, 1984, International Bible Society. Used by permission of Zondervan Bible Publishers. Other versions used are: the *King James Version* (KJV); the *New American Standard Bible* (NASB), © The Lockman Foundation, 1960, 1962, 1963, 1968, 1971, 1972, 1973, 1975, 1977; and *The Living Bible* (TLB), copyright 1971 by Tyndale House Publishers, Wheaton, IL, used by permission.

Printed in the United States of America

9 10 11 12 13 14 15 16 17/99 98 97 96 95 94

Contents

*This book is dedicated
to my precious wife, Christie,
whose encouragement and love
have been gifts from God
to stir my own growth
and develop my vision for His world.*

Author

Paul Borthwick is the Minister of Missions at Grace Chapel in Lexington, Massachusetts. Paul has served there since 1971 as a volunteer, singles director, youth pastor, and now as missions pastor. He and his wife, Christie, have coordinated over sixty cross-cultural service teams for youth and adults since 1978. These teams—as well as their personal ministries— have enabled the Borthwicks to learn from and serve with missions ministries in Latin America, Europe, Africa, and Asia.

Paul is the author of three other books and a variety of articles on topics related to youth and missions. He and his wife, Christie, live in Lexington.

Acknowledgments

This book is a product of the accumulated effect of others on my life. Through the teaching, example, and stimulation of others, I have been forced to develop my own "mind for missions," and I am indebted to these people.

Various teachers and authors have been sources of inspiration and challenge. Of the many who have affected me, Gordon MacDonald, David Howard, John Stott, Ralph Winter, Elisabeth Elliot, and J. Christy Wilson stand out in their impact on my life and vision.

The more notable people, however, are those alongside whom I have had the privilege of working and growing here at Grace Chapel. Fellow staff members, elders, missions committee members, youth leaders, and summer mission team members have all served to bolster my world vision. The people who stand out include Larry Anzivino, Dan Dustin, Mary Ann Mitchener, Steve Macchia, Margaret Hunt, Tim Conder, Jimmy Dodd, and Dan Mahoney. I thank God for their impact on me.

Finally, I am grateful to my faithful and diligent secretary, Cathy Franzoni, who typed this manuscript during her free time. Her commitment to excellence in her "behind-the-scenes" work in missions has greatly benefited our church's involvement in the Great Commission.

Foreword

We have but one life to invest for God. In *A Mind for Missions*, Paul Borthwick explains how to make the most of our time here on earth prior to standing before the judgment seat of Christ to give account of what we have done (see 2 Corinthians 5:10). Many believers are "worldly Christians." In the pages that follow, we have a guide to the way we can become "world Christians" through fulfilling the purpose God has for us. We are challenged to give our lives to the Lord as a "blank check" for Him to work out His will in us. Robert Moffat, the father-in-law of David Livingstone, said, "We have all eternity in which to enjoy our victories, but only one short life in which to win them."

As Minister of Missions at Grace Chapel in Lexington, Massachusetts, the writer of this volume is not just theoretical but practical as well in his presentation. He and his wife, Christie, have organized scores of teams from their congregation to go as short-term missionaries to many parts of the world. Paul and Christie have accompanied some of the teams. Furthermore, the author teaches a challenging course at Gordon-Conwell on "Missions and the Local Church," a course that stimulates those enrolled in it to build a world vision.

A Mind for Missions deals with the greatest need of today. God's method for evangelizing the world is through people. The Bible promises that "the earth will be filled with the knowledge of the glory of the LORD, as the waters cover the sea" (Habakkuk 2:14). In this book, Paul Borthwick demonstrates the way in which world Christians can be trained and become "workers together with God" in completing Christ's commission.

J. Christy Wilson, Jr.
Professor of World Evangelization
Gordon-Conwell Theological Seminary

Introduction

When Jesus invited His first disciples to follow Him (Matthew 4:19), He asked them to make a commitment. Today the Lord Jesus Christ issues the same invitation to each of us, but—as with that first invitation—He asks us to make a commitment. Jerry White, General Director of The Navigators, explains the nature of the commitment Christ asks us to make:

> We make the commitment and leave the results to God. In a sense, it's like signing a blank check and allowing God to fill in the amount. It can be a frightening adventure. But God will never demand more from us than we have to give.[1]

After we make the basic decision to follow Jesus Christ and give Him that "blank check," we still face many choices in our daily discipleship. One of the most basic choices is where we will focus our attention, whether we will focus on ourselves or on the world around us. Expressed another way, we face a choice to be *worldly Christians* or *world Christians.*

A worldly Christian is one who accepts the basic message of salvation, but whose lifestyle, priorities, and concerns are molded by self-centered preoccupation. The selfish spirit of our age leads the worldly Christian to look to God and the Bible primarily for personal fulfillment. The worldly Christian looks to Scripture for personal blessing; prays mostly for immediate, personal needs; and sees the Christian faith as a way to "get God on his or her side."

The worldly Christian's desire for self-fulfillment or personal satisfaction makes his or her perspective very narrow. As such, he or she may oppose a worldwide perspective, and can actually oppose the worldwide commission of the gospel. Even nonbelievers recognize such narrow thinking as being harmful to worldwide objectives. The late Chinese leader Mao Tse-tung spoke to the problem of the self-centered person in his vision: "Whenever the mind becomes rigid, it is very dangerous."[2]

The worldly Christian *is* rigid in his or her thinking. The mind is closed to certain aspects of God's revealed will, and attention turns inward. Missions expert J. Herbert Kane summarized the worldly Christian's problem this way:

> Everybody prides himself in having an open mind, but few actually achieve it. Man's capacity for self-deception is enormous. We think we have an open mind while in fact we are victims of our own prejudices and predilections. We have long ago decided that there are certain things we will not do. We wouldn't dare say it to God, but in our minds we have decided, "Anything but Christian service," or "Anywhere but the foreign field."[3]

As Christians, we face the choice: Will we turn inward and focus on the new life we have in Christ only as it benefits us? Or will we look beyond ourselves, opening ourselves completely to God and His purposes for us?

As Jerry White stated, giving God the "blank check" of

our lives can be a frightening adventure because He may work in ways that we are not used to. Like the Apostle Peter in Acts 10, we may find God at work in ways that are beyond our normal (and sometimes self-centered) ways of thinking. Yet if we open ourselves to God and overcome our selfishness, we can embark on the great adventure of becoming *world Christians.* A world Christian breaks the mold of a self-centered way of thinking. A world Christian understands that Jesus calls us to deny ourselves (Luke 9:23) so that we might respond to a world of greater need beyond ourselves. As David Bryant says, "World Christians are day-to-day disciples for whom Christ's global cause has become the integrating, overriding priority for all that He is for them. Like disciples should, they actively investigate all that their Master's Great Commission means. Then they act on what they learn. World Christians are Christians whose life directions have been solidly transformed by a world vision."[4]

Becoming a world Christian or a worldly Christian is a choice we all face. Realistically, choosing the self-centered, worldly route will cost us greatly in our discipleship (if indeed we can even consider ourselves disciples when our eyes are narrowly focused on ourselves to the exclusion of others!). A self-centered focus will lead us away from understanding God's greatness. On the other hand, choosing a world focus will expand our vision, open our minds and hearts, and help us understand the greatness of our God in a way we have never before experienced.

NO REAL OPTION

Actually, the choice to become a world Christian is not really a choice at all if we desire healthy discipleship. Missions expert Peter Wagner explains the Christian's choice this way:

Some things in life are optional and some are not. Wearing shoes is optional. But eating is not.

Driving a car is optional. But once you choose the option, driving on the right-hand side of the road (here in America) is not.

Becoming a Christian is optional. But once you decide to ask Jesus Christ to take control of your life, involvement in world missions is no longer optional.

I'm not saying that these things are impossible. You can choose to go without eating, but if you do you must take the consequences. You must be willing to exist at a low energy level, to invite infection and disease, and if you persist, to die.

You can choose to drive on the left but you will pay fines and cause accidents.[5]

To focus our attention outward, to grow as world Christians, is really not an option at all. Looking to the needs, concerns, and opportunities of our world in the same way that our Lord would is a basic part of identifying ourselves with Him. If we choose to live with no outward focus, we will suffer. Peter Wagner identifies three realms where our spiritual growth will be hampered if we choose to be worldly Christians:

You can reject missions even if you are a Christian. But the consequences are clear:

1. You will find yourself sitting on the bench while you could be in there playing the game . . . missions are on the cutting edge of excitement in the Christian life. Being left out means a dull existence as a child of God. It is less than God's best for you.

2. You will lose authenticity as a Christian. You say that Jesus is your Lord, but yet you will be failing

to obey Him at a crucial point. Another word for that is hypocrisy.

    3. You will be poorly prepared for that judgment day when what we have done here on earth will be tested by fire and only the gold, silver, and precious stones will survive (1 Corinthians 3:12-15).[6]

HOW DOES ONE BECOME A WORLD CHRISTIAN?

In order to become world Christians, we must learn to combat the overwhelming spirit of selfishness that we see through the media, through popular opinion, and even through aberrant doctrines that are being taught in Christian churches. The most basic way to do this is to start seeing the world as God sees it. We must believe that "the origin of missions is *ultimately* to be found in the heart of God. . . . No thought of God is true to His revelation of Himself that does not rest on the fact that He 'so loved the world that He gave His only begotten Son' that by believing in Him 'the world should be saved through Him.'"[7]

    This truth transformed the Apostle Paul, Francis Xavier, Hudson Taylor, Bob Pierce, and Billy Graham. This truth can transform us, too. When we start to see the world with Christ's love and compassion (in the words of Bob Pierce, to have our hearts "broken with the things that break the heart of God"), our perspective enlarges. Like David, we will say, "I will run the way of Thy commandments, for Thou will enlarge my heart" (Psalm 119:32, NASB).

    Seeking God's perspective on the world can quickly overwhelm us, however, if we are not focusing our attention on Him. Only He can love *the world*; we do not have that capacity. This need to focus first on God is why the leaders of WORLDTEAM challenge those who would be world Christians to remember that, "for the World Christian, life begins with God, not the world around him, nor even the need of world evangelism. He is absorbed first in God and for that reason he becomes absorbed with humanity. The World Christian takes up the case of world missions because he understands that to be God's cause. Because 'God so loved the world,' the World Christian absorbed in God is committed to His program of world redemption."[8]

I am so far from this ideal, you may think. *I want to see the world from God's perspective, and I want to be so absorbed in God that I am likewise absorbed in His purposes, but I am not there yet.* Take heart! None of us has arrived. None of us are fully world Christians, but we can choose to grow in that direction.

If we desire to become world Christians, we need to choose to start formulating a world view that is honoring to God and consistent with His worldwide purposes:

> Anthropologists . . . explain that at our cores is a basic view of reality—a worldview. That worldview determines who we are, what we will value, and how we behave.
>
> If our worldview is unChristian, or less-than-biblical, it will inevitably surface in values and actions that contradict the heart of the biblical worldview. . . .
>
> But if my actions stem from a biblical worldview, then it becomes a matter of *faithful obedience.* I can allow a fad to slip away, but not something that goes as deep as obedience. I have decided to follow Jesus with my whole life, and I understand where He's going. It's no longer a matter of choosing a career or lifestyle—it's a matter of faithfulness.[9]

The choice to grow, therefore, is basic to our starting the process of developing biblical world visions. To be faithful in that which we learn is also basic, but there is more.

If we are going to go forward as world Christians and be stretched by an expanding view of God's world, we must make two more choices.

First, we must determine to get our eyes off ourselves. Like the Apostle Paul, we must say, "I no longer live, but Christ lives in me" (Galatians 2:20), and "If we live, we live to the Lord" (Romans 14:8). Our lives are not our own. We have been "bought at a price" (1 Corinthians 6:20), and our goal is to grow as disciples—those who choose to be identified with the Lord Jesus Christ.

In practical terms, this may mean overcoming our fear of others and sharing the gospel with peers or coworkers. It may mean revising our sleeping, eating, or spending habits. Whatever it means to each of us, it is a conscious statement to ourselves that we are going to allow Jesus to be our *Lord.*

Second, we must build for growth. All of us realize that we are far from our goal of being world Christians, both in terms of personal worship of our great God and in terms of our obedience to His calling into the world around us. But we can grow!

Building world vision in ourselves and others means that we grow toward God's goal that every people and tongue and nation would worship Him (Revelation 7:9-10) by starting right where we are. In the process of building a world vision, we may become discouraged when we see how far we have yet to go, but we can also turn around and be encouraged by how far we have come.

Developing a world vision does not mean that we forget about the people around us. It does not mean that we become preoccupied with the people "over there" (a phenomenon Eugene Peterson calls "Afghanistanitis," the belief that the real needs are all beyond us), nor does it mean we pack our belongings and head to the airport while praying for

God to direct us to the "right" plane to take overseas. We must not neglect the need and mandate to be witnesses right where we are. As our worldwide compassion for the lost builds, we must demonstrate this compassion to friends, relatives, and neighbors—people God has put in our lives right now. Reaching out to those who are near us will remind us of the millions around the world who have no opportunity to hear of Christ and will challenge us to pray and act.

LET'S START BUILDING!

The challenge of becoming world Christians lies before us. Knowing that we displease the Lord when we choose a worldly Christian attitude and lifestyle, may we choose instead the countercultural option of the world Christian.

Becoming world Christians is a lifelong process, but there are certain building blocks that will help us in our growth. This book suggests ten building blocks through which a world Christian vision can be enhanced and enlarged.

Building a world vision, however, is still a challenge. It requires discipline, hard work, and the willingness to fight against our own self-centeredness. "Admiral Mahon of the American Navy during the War of Independence is said to have insisted on a dictum when teaching his officers: 'Gentlemen, whenever you set out to accomplish anything, make up your mind at the outset about your ultimate objective. Once you have decided on it, take care never to lose sight of it.'"[10] Let us not lose sight of our goal of becoming world Christians!

NOTES:
1. Jerry White, *The Power of Commitment* (Colorado Springs, Colorado: NavPress, 1984), page 48.

2. Quoted in Orville Schell, *In the People's Republic* (New York: Random House, 1977), page 49.
3. J. Herbert Kane, *Life and Work on the Mission Field* (Grand Rapids, Michigan: Baker Book House, 1980), page 8.
4. David Bryant, *In the Gap* (Downers Grove, Illinois: InterVarsity Press, 1979), page 73.
5. Peter Wagner, *On the Crest of the Wave* (Ventura, California: Regal Books, 1983), page 5.
6. Wagner, page 6.
7. William Owen Carver, "The Missionary Idea in the Bible," *Classics in Christian Missions* (Nashville, Tennessee: Broadman Press, 1979), page 32.
8. *What Does It Mean to Be a World Christian?* (Coral Gables, Florida: WORLD-TEAM, 1978), page 7.
9. Sam Wilson and Gordon Aeschliman, *The Hidden Half* (Monrovia, California: MARC, n.d.), page 97.
10. Quoted in John White, *Excellence in Leadership* (Downers Grove, Illinois: InterVarsity Press, 1986), page 73.

The Scriptures

At an Urbana Missionary Conference put on by InterVarsity Christian Fellowship, the 15,000 students and missionaries in the huge auditorium of the University of Illinois hummed with anticipation and excitement in preparation for the first of several biblical expositions on missions from British scholar and Christian leader, Dr. John R.W. Stott. After his introduction, Dr. Stott stepped to the podium. To my surprise, he asked us to turn to the Old Testament—to Genesis 12.

I cannot remember all that Dr. Stott said that day, or in the days to come, but two things lodged fast in my mind that week. First, he stated a number of times that "our God is a missionary God." Second, he showed us this from the Old Testament.

These two points stayed with me because they opened my mind to the fact that missions is not an addendum that God had Jesus command His followers to pursue just before He left the earth. Instead, missions comes from the heart of God. The message of missions is woven throughout the Bible, and the sending of God's people into all the earth was not an appendix to the story of redemption. Missions was in God's heart all along. Our God is a missionary God!

Many people who think themselves to be "missions

minded" still need to look at the whole of Scripture to see God's entire witness. Missions is not a New Testament idea; it permeates Scripture. A careful study of Scripture reveals God's consistent, purposeful, and merciful desire to see all peoples come into fellowship with Him. Missions leader David Howard explains the scriptural foundation of missions this way:

> The missionary enterprise of the church is not a pyramid built upside down with its point on one isolated text in the New Testament out of which we have built a huge structure known as "missions." Rather, the missionary enterprise of the church is a great pyramid built right side up with its base running from Genesis 1 to Revelation 22. All of Scripture forms the foundation for the outreach of the gospel to the whole world.[1]

What better place to start, then, than with Scripture as we seek to build our world vision? The Bible promises that it is profitable for our "training in righteousness" (2 Timothy 3:16), and if developing our world vision is part of that training, we must start in God's revealed Word.

We must be willing, however, to open our eyes so we can see God's Word in a way we have never seen it before. We can study the Bible with a self-centered focus, which may help us in personal growth, but we must take our self-oriented blinders off to understand God's whole counsel and realize the full effect of God's revelation of Himself as the "missionary God."

Our self-centered focus in Bible study, according to Martin Goldsmith, is one of the failures of contemporary churches:

> Why do many ministers fail to teach world mission in their regular Bible exposition? Why do students fail to

pass on this vision to new Christians? Why do many Christians of all ages consider overseas mission to be an optional extra? The fundamental reason is that they do not see it as a basic teaching of the whole of Scripture. It is a failure to grasp the biblical basis of mission that stops it being taught in the normal everyday programme of Bible teaching.[2]

With our eyes open wide, then, let us take a look at the scriptural witness.

THE OLD TESTAMENT WITNESS

Creation. The book of Genesis opens us to what scholar Johannes Verkuyl calls the "universal motif"[3] of the Old Testament. Through Genesis we see that God created the heavens and the earth. He is introduced as the Lord and Maker of all creation. "The relation of God to the world is not the relation of cause to its effect," writes William Dyrness. "The relation is rather one of a personal Creator to his creation."[4] God is personally interested in all of His creation, not just one group of people or one isolated geographic area.

From out of His creation, God created His ultimate masterpiece—mankind. In his prefallen state, this perfect man was given a commission, which theologians call the "cultural mandate," to "be fruitful and increase in number; fill the earth and subdue it" (Genesis 1:28). Man was also instructed to enjoy all of creation in its "vast array" (Genesis 2:1).

But then Adam and Eve sinned. God, in His desire to have worshipers and not puppets, had given them the freedom to choose, and they chose to disobey God. Because of their disobedience, fellowship with God was broken and God's perfect creation was marred by imperfection.

Yet even in the crisis of Adam and Eve's sin, the fact that God is a missionary God is evident. Although their fellowship was broken, God sought out His created beings in order to demonstrate His desire for reconciliation and redemption: "But the LORD God called to the man, 'Where are you?'" (Genesis 3:9).

So from the Fall onward, God has been seeking to call men and women back to Himself. In Genesis 3:21 we read that "the LORD God made garments of skin for Adam and his wife and clothed them." As the making of the garments foreshadowed, God was willing to shed blood so that the effects of sin could be covered.

Our God is a missionary God. He demonstrated this in His creation and in His pursuit of man after the Fall.

Abraham. As a result of Adam's sin, human civilization began outside of fellowship with God. Humanity populated the earth, fulfilling the mandate found in Genesis 1:28, but without God's intended perfection. So in time God destroyed the earth because of man's wickedness (Genesis 6:5-6), but He redeemed Noah and his family because of their righteousness (Genesis 7:1). Later, confusion reigned at the Tower of Babel (Genesis 11).

Yet in the midst of this profusion of sin, and out of the increased distance that was building between God and man, God called Abram (Genesis 12:1-3). God made a covenant with Abram, promising him that he would be the agent of God's redemption to all the earth. Through Abram God promised that "all peoples on earth will be blessed" (Genesis 12:3).

Dr. John Stott explains the significance of this covenant:

There is but one living and true God, the Creator of the universe, the Lord of the nations and the God of the spirits of all flesh. Some 4,000 years ago he called

Abraham and made a covenant with him, promising not only to bless him but also through his posterity to bless all the families of the earth. This biblical text is one of the foundation stones of the Christian mission. For Abraham's descendants (through whom all nations are being blessed) are Christ and the people of Christ. If by faith we belong to Christ, we are Abraham's spiritual children and have a responsibility to all mankind.[5]

God's call to Abraham is repeated in Genesis 17:1-7, where God establishes the "everlasting covenant" with Abraham and his descendants. Through Abraham and his descendants, God again took the initiative to bring His blessing and redemption to all the earth.

The Law. God wanted to bring His message of blessing and redemption to all the earth through Abraham's physical descendants, the people of Israel. But their sinfulness required the establishment of the Law.

Even in the Law, which is usually considered to be a revelation specifically for the people of Israel, God demonstrates His love for all who are not redeemed. At the outset of the Ten Commandments, God establishes that there is one God in all the earth: "You shall have no other gods before me" (Exodus 20:3). The people of Israel were called to be witnesses of this one true God: "Israel wasn't great because of the number of people or the wars it won or the cities it built—Israel was great because God called the nation to demonstrate His character and love to the nations around it."[6] Thus the righteousness of the Law was intended to set Israel apart (see Leviticus 20:22-26; Deuteronomy 7:6-8, 14:2, 28:1). Later God made it plain that Israel's selection was to lead others to "acknowledge the LORD" (Isaiah 19:21), but the initial call of the mission was that one nation would know Him.

In the Law, God also actively reminds the Israelites to be concerned and compassionate toward the "aliens and strangers" because they themselves had been aliens in Egypt when God redeemed them (see Exodus 22:21, Leviticus 19:33-34, Deuteronomy 10:17-19).

The Law, then, witnesses to the fact that the descendants of Abraham—through whom all the nations of the earth were to be blessed—were to be set apart. They were to live out the righteousness of the one true God whose glory they were to declare in the whole earth (see Numbers 14:21, Deuteronomy 28:10).

The prophets. When the people of Israel rebelled against God, He raised up prophets as "missionaries, echoing the call of God."[7] The earlier prophets—like Elijah and Elisha—stood before rebellious and pagan kings, exhorted them to worship the one true God, and handed down God's judgment on those who chose to rebel. The later prophets spoke and wrote as God's voice, calling the people back into fellowship with Him. Their purpose in restoring the people of Israel to fellowship with God was so that the Israelites could be God's witnesses in the world.

William Dyrness clarifies the prophets' purpose:

> By the time we come to the prophets it is clear that the calling of Israel as a nation is for the sake of the whole world . . . Israel then is to be preserved (cf. Esther) so that she can mediate God's promises for his creation as a whole. They are to exhibit a people, institutions, and a land which will reflect God's glory so that this can one day be communicated to the whole earth and to all peoples.[8]

With God's redemptive purpose clearly in mind, the prophets spoke and wrote. Isaiah spoke with the vision that "the whole earth is full of his glory" (Isaiah 6:3) and predicted, like Habakkuk in Habakkuk 2:14, that the day would come when "the earth will be full of the knowledge of the LORD as the waters cover the sea" (Isaiah 11:9). Through Isaiah, God promised the people of Israel that they would be "a covenant for the people and a light for the Gentiles" (Isaiah 42:6; see also 60:3). In Isaiah 52:10 we plainly see God's worldwide purpose: "The LORD will lay bare his holy arm in the sight of all the nations, and all the ends of the earth will see the salvation of our God" (see also Isaiah 45:22-23).

While Isaiah is the most outspoken prophet regarding God's commission to the people of Israel to be a "light of revelation to the Gentiles," others like Habakkuk and Micah echo the same message. In Micah 5:4-5, for example, we read, "And they will live securely, for then his greatness will reach to the ends of the earth. And he will be their peace."

The psalms. The writers of the psalms likewise reflect a worldwide understanding of God's purposes. When referring to God at work in the world, their overriding theme was that God's name should be declared in all the earth. For example, in Psalm 33:8 we see that all the earth is urged to worship God; in Psalm 67:1-2 God is asked to work in such a way that His power and His name would be known throughout the earth; in Psalm 96:3 God's worshipers are exhorted to be witnesses to God's glory throughout the whole earth; and in Psalm 145:8-13 the psalmist testifies that God's people will themselves speak of God in such a way that "all men may know of your mighty acts" (verse 12).

The declaration of God's name throughout the earth is ultimately summed up in Psalm 2:8, which is a prophecy of God's work through Jesus Christ: "Ask of me, and I will make the nations your inheritance, the ends of the earth your possession."

Missionaries. The Old Testament's "universal motif" is

demonstrated not only through the Scriptures themselves, but also through the people presented in Scripture. Elisha's work, for example, demonstrated God's redemption to Gentiles like the Shunammite woman (2 Kings 4:8ff) and Naaman the Syrian (2 Kings 5). Esther served as God's missionary to her Gentile captors, and Joseph was God's agent of redemption in Egypt (Genesis 50:20). The fact that God is a missionary God, however, is nowhere more evident in the Old Testament then in the lives of Daniel and Jonah, two "witnesses" to pagan kingdoms.

As God's messenger, Daniel's ministry brought him in touch with four pagan kings—Nebuchadnezzar, Belshazzar, Cyrus, and Darius. Daniel's witness was consistent and convicting, to the point that Nebuchadnezzar of Babylon was seemingly converted (Daniel 4:34-37). Daniel himself saw the universal aspect of God's dominion in a vision where "one like a son of man" was given "authority, glory and sovereign power; all peoples, nations and men of every language worshiped him" (Daniel 7:13-14). Perhaps the greatest testimony to Daniel's work as a missionary in a pagan land occurred after God's hand saved him from the lions. When King Darius saw what Daniel's God had done, he ordered "all the peoples, nations and men of every language throughout the land" to "fear and reverence the God of Daniel" (Daniel 6:25-27). In these instances, God worked to bring His redemption to nonIsraelites through one Israelite who was being a "light to the nations" as God intended.

Another Old Testament messenger who served as a missionary, although not quite as willingly as Daniel, was Jonah. Called to be a missionary to Nineveh, Jonah first ran from God's call. Through the influence of a storm, three days in the belly of a great fish, and direct confrontation with God, Jonah became convinced that he should go to Nineveh as a missionary, which was what God originally intended.

In Nineveh, Jonah preached and achieved great results. The whole city, under the leadership of the king and his nobles, repented. God had mercy and spared the city. There were hundreds—maybe thousands—of converts, yet Jonah became depressed (Jonah 4). Jonah explained his depression in a prayer to God, "I knew that you are a gracious and compassionate God, slow to anger and abounding in love, a God who relents from sending calamity" (Jonah 4:2). Jonah knew the character of the God of the Old Testament; he knew that God would send him as an agent of redemption to save the people of Nineveh (who were probably Jonah's natural enemies). Jonah knew God's character and knew that God wanted to show mercy to all peoples and nations. Although Jonah did not like God's plan to bring redemption to all peoples, he was compelled to be a messenger of God's redemption.

Summary. Our God is a missionary God. He prepared His people Israel, as children of Abraham, to be a blessing to all nations. In the Old Testament, God's people made choices that kept them from fulfilling His perfect plan, but they could not stop His purposes from being plainly stated. God was in the business of redemption, and He would accomplish His purposes through His Messiah. As William Dyrness observes, "The Old Testament prepares a universal message for what will become in the New Testament a universal mission."[9]

THE NEW TESTAMENT WITNESS

The Messiah has come. God's ways are perfect, and despite the rebellion of the people of Israel, He accomplished His purpose through Abraham's seed. Jesus Christ, who is the promised Messiah—the fulfillment of Old Testament prophecy—came out of the nation of Israel so that the light of revelation could come to the Gentiles, enabling all nations to be blessed through Abraham.

The gospels. The message of the gospels, that Jesus came for the whole world, is plain. It is seen from the appearance of the wise men of the East at Jesus' crib to Jesus' affinity for Samaritans, Gentiles, and other undesirables. Luke's gospel documents the Messiah's outreach to the centurion (Luke 7:1-10) and others who were not acceptable to the religious leaders of the day. John shows Jesus interacting with a Samaritan woman of ill repute (John 4). Matthew documents Jesus' compassion for a Canaanite woman (Matthew 15:21-28) as does Mark in Mark 7:24-30.

Beyond His personal example of involvement with non-Jews, Jesus also told parables to let the religious leaders know that God's favor had fallen to others and not to them. Jesus defied the expectations of many regarding the Messiah by summarizing His mission with the words, "The Son of Man came to seek and to save what was lost" (Luke 19:10).

Through His Son, God demonstrates His sending heart; He reaches out to lost humanity by giving the only sacrifice that will satisfy the Law and restore a right relationship between man and God. Jesus Christ, God's divine Son, is sent so that "whoever believes in him shall not perish but have eternal life" (John 3:16).

In the gospels, the missionary God reveals Himself through His Son who is not only sent, but also sends His followers with a renewed commission to which the people of Israel never obediently responded. The commission is clear—so clear that all four gospel writers recorded it in one form or another (and Luke recorded it again in Acts 1:8):

Matthew 28:19—"Therefore go and make disciples of all the nations."
Mark 16:15—"Go into all the world and preach the good news to all creation."

Luke 24:47—"Repentance and forgiveness of sins will be preached in his name to all nations."

John 20:21—"As the Father has sent me, I am sending you."

Acts. World missions is at the center of this historical account of the start of the Church. Acts begins with a reiteration of Jesus' commission, only it refers to the *power* of the witness as well as the location of the witness. Acts 1:8 identifies the Holy Spirit as the sending force behind the missionaries as they go out into their own community (Jerusalem), their region (all Judea), the region that was socially and ethnically different from their own (Samaria), and the world beyond their knowledge (the ends of the earth).

In Acts we see that the mission of the Church was no longer in the hands of the divine Son. Through the Holy Spirit, it was entrusted to human beings who were sent into the world as witnesses—heralds of God's grace. Since these witnesses had touched, experienced, and felt His grace (1 John 1:1), they could testify to it. Acts reveals the Church's proper response to the Great Commission. The Christians undertook the fulfillment of the commission as a "responsibility which was to be shouldered by every member."[10]

Yet the early Christians were far from perfect. In Acts 8:1 we see that it took persecution to scatter the Church out of Jerusalem into the world, and Acts 10 shows that even the leaders of the Church were hesitant to open their doors to Gentiles. But as the Holy Spirit continued to work the gospel went out, documenting that God indeed was no respecter of persons "but accepts men from every nation who fear him and do what is right" (Acts 10:35).

The Epistles. Some people argue against missions because of the apparent lack of missions-oriented references in the Epistles. Such arguing, however, ignores one very significant aspect of the letters' contexts; they are basically missionary letters written from a missionary (or missionaries) to young Christians who were becoming established in the faith.

The Epistles were written from missionaries to mission-planted churches in order to address problems in the early Church (1 Corinthians, Galatians) or to establish an understanding of the gospel of Jesus Christ (Romans, Galatians). Some epistles address the theology of the Church or church structure (Ephesians, the Pastoral Epistles), while others console Christians who face hardship (Peter's letters). The supremacy of Christ (Hebrews), personal issues (Philemon), and encouragement (Philippians) are among other topics dealt with in the New Testament missionary letters. However, each epistle reiterates Scripture's message that God wants "all men to be saved and to come to a knowledge of the truth" (1 Timothy 2:4; see also 2 Peter 3:9).

Revelation. The mysterious last book of the Bible has challenged scholars and theologians for centuries. Symbolism, imagery, and hidden meanings make it difficult to interpret, but the image of the missionary God of Scripture is nevertheless plain. Revelation portrays God as the sovereign ruler of history. At the end of time, people from the ends of the earth will offer their worship to Him. "After this I looked and there before me was a great multitude that no one could count, from every nation, tribe, people, and language, standing before the throne and in front of the Lamb. They were wearing white robes and were holding palm branches in their hands. And they cried out in a loud voice, 'Salvation belongs to our God, who sits on the throne, and to the Lamb'" (Revelation 7:9-10).

Summary. Throughout the New Testament, the missionary God of the Old Testament continues His redemptive work through His Son and Church by the power of His Holy Spirit. As Stott observes, the theme of being sent on a mission intensifies in the New Testament: "The primal mission is God's, for it is he who sent his prophets, his Son, his Spirit. Of these missions, the mission of the Son is central, for it was the culmination of the ministry of the prophets, and it embraced within itself as its climax the sending of the Spirit. *And now the Son sends as he himself was sent*"[11] (emphasis added).

The New Testament's message is that the missionary God of the Old Testament has come, in the form of a man, that He might bring redemption to the creation that chose to disobey Him. But there is more. To those who receive salvation from the divine Redeemer sent from God, there is a commission to take that message to all the world. It is on this biblical theme of sending that we build our vision.

THE DOMINANT THEMES IN SCRIPTURE

If we are striving to increase our world vision, what does Scripture teach us? There are at least three dominant themes in the Bible that we must focus on if we are to have a correct world vision: there is salvation in no one else; the basis of mission is to reveal the glory of God; and God wants to use us. Let's consider each of these themes separately.

There is salvation in no one else. The witness of Scripture is our greatest motivation for missions, and Scripture clearly teaches that there is no salvation apart from the God of Israel and no redemption outside of His Son, Jesus Christ.

Throughout the Bible, God's uniqueness and the uniqueness of Jesus Christ as *Savior* is clear. While the God of the Old Testament takes the initiative toward sinful man, He will in no way tolerate other gods (Exodus 20:3), nor will He share His glory with any others (Isaiah 42:8 and 48:11). He declares, "Apart from me there is no savior" (Isaiah 43:11), and says that at His name every knee shall bow (Isaiah 45:23).

The unique theme of salvation through the one true God

of Scripture continues into the New Testament, where Jesus Christ—the incarnate God—is revealed. "No one comes to the Father except through me" (John 14:6) is Jesus' echo of Isaiah 43:11. The apostles reflect their understanding of salvation through Christ alone when they state emphatically, "There is salvation in no one else" (Acts 4:12). Paul shows the same understanding of salvation when he writes, "There is one God and one mediator between God and men, the man Christ Jesus" (1 Timothy 2:5). He again portrays his understanding of Jesus as the only Savior when he writes, "At the name of Jesus every knee should bow" (Philippians 2:10), which is a New Testament interpretation of Isaiah 45:23.

Why is this emphasis on Jesus as our only Savior important? Simply because the fact that Jesus Christ is the only way to God and there is no salvation apart from the God of Scripture is our basic motivation for missions. If there are other ways to God or other "mediators," then we have no reason to develop a world vision. If there are many ways to God or many ways to obtain salvation, then we have no reason to bother with missions at all. (And, Jesus would have had no reason to come to earth.)

In his fine book, *The Great Omission,* Dr. J. Robertson McQuilkin attributes our failure to fulfill the Great Commission to errant doctrine regarding Jesus as our only salvation. The "wider hope" theory—that there might be other ways to God outside of Jesus Christ—diminishes any incentive to spread the gospel. If sincerity saves, then people have no need for Jesus as long as they are sincere in whatever they believe. If people can be saved through general, universal salvation—the belief that Christ's death saves people even if they do not know of or believe in Him—then there is no need to send missionaries, support missionaries, or pray for them.[12] The study of Scripture, however, reveals a different theological and world view altogether: there is one God; He has come to us to redeem us in the Person of Jesus Christ; there is salvation in no one else. Although we may want to subscribe to some "wider hope" theories, doing so requires us to deny the clear, salvation message of the Old and New Testaments.

The basis of mission is to reveal the glory of God. Scripture teaches that there is one all-powerful, all-glorious, perfect, and holy God who desires that all of His creation experience His glory. But through Adam's sin, His creation has fallen, and now the glorious God seeks our redemption. This means that the work of missions is God's. He will work to accomplish His purposes (see Isaiah 55:11 and Daniel 4:35). He chooses to use us, but is not dependent on us (see Job 38:4, Isaiah 66:1-2, and Luke 17:10). God is not in a rush; He has not lost control of the world; His ultimate purposes are not being thwarted; He is still all-powerful, all-glorious, and still seeks to bring humanity back to Himself so that we might experience His glory (see 2 Corinthians 4:6).

The great missionary to the North American Indians, David Brainerd, knew this glorious God of the Bible. His vision of God motivated his vision for missions: "Brainerd prays for his friends and his enemies. But this act of prayer rises out of a higher vision. God must be known, and not simply by name. God's name was well-known, even in the wilds of New Jersey. God must be known as GOD! To Brainerd that was the great thing. Even Christ's kingdom serves that end. Let God be known! To know God is the great essential. And to make him known was Brainerd's task."[13]

A.W. Tozer, a great leader and writer from the Christian and Missionary Alliance, was fully committed to a missions vision, but feared that through our efforts to exhort action in missions we would diminish the worship of the Almighty. He wrote, "We commonly represent God as a busy, eager, somewhat frustrated Father hurrying about seeking help to carry out His benevolent plan to bring peace and salvation to the world. . . . Too many missionary appeals are based upon this fancied frustration of Almighty God."[14] Tozer is saying, in effect, "Don't get interested in missions out of some delusion that God is in trouble. He is still the Creator of the ends of the earth, the great Redeemer, the Almighty."

Serious study of Scripture helps keep our perspective straight. Scripture reveals that the one true God calls us into missions to declare His glory. Therefore, knowing Him is our top priority, and making Him known is then a natural result.

God wants to use us. The point Tozer made teaches us that God does not *need* our help. Yet Scripture reminds us that God, in His divine mercy and grace, *chooses* to use us (see Jeremiah 29:11, 1 Corinthians 15:10, and 1 Peter 2:4-10). This message from Scripture transformed Cameron Townsend. Through Scripture, he saw not only salvation's plan, but also saw a vision of how God would use him.

From childhood, Cam Townsend had studied Scripture: "All his life Cam had been a man of one book—the Bible. He recalls how every weekday morning before milking his father would read three chapters—five on Sunday. After breakfast came family devotions—Bible reading, a hymn, and prayers. . . . He (Townsend's father, Will) always ended his prayers with, 'May the knowledge of the Lord cover the earth as the waters cover the sea.'"[15] In the process of growing in his knowledge of God—perhaps as he heard about Joseph, Daniel, Jonah, Paul, and Peter—Cam Townsend became convinced that God wanted to use him. Thus, when he was challenged by a Cakchiquel Indian from Guatemala in 1917 who asked, "If your God is so great, why can't He talk our Cakchiquel language?" Townsend was ready to act.[16] "Uncle Cam," as he became known, founded Wycliffe Bible Translators and was used mightily by God to bring His Word to many tribes and peoples. The testimony of Scripture reveals that God can use any person who yields his or her life to Him.

BUILD YOUR WORLD VISION WITH SCRIPTURE!

From Genesis to Revelation, from Creation to the end of human history, God desires fellowship with man, His creation. God's redemptive work is evident from His initial seeking after man following the Fall (Genesis 3:9ff) to the covenants He made with Noah and Abraham, from the people of faith to the work of the Cross. His love is worldwide, His love is active, His love is redemptive: "God so loved the world that he gave his one and only Son" (John 3:16).

The Scriptures are the first world vision building block because God uses these words to change us. As we let the words of Scripture do their work by the power of the Holy Spirit, our view of God, our view of the world, and our view of ourselves change. We see the eternal, omnipotent Creator as Lord of the universe. His creation, most notably humankind, is the target of His love, and we are agents of His love. Jesus' commissions in Matthew 28:18-20 and Acts 1:8 become the launching pads from which we take off with a knowledge of a great God and His worldwide plan.

As William Carey, the "father of modern missions," read the Bible, "he became convinced that foreign missions were the central responsibility of the church."[17] Dawson Trotman, founder of The Navigators, developed his world vision by reading the Bible and shared his vision with others: "Daws' method of instilling world vision was to lay a foundation from the Bible, for he knew that a challenge with any lesser authority would soon evaporate and become a forgotten emotion."[18]

Dr. John Stott summarizes our need to know God well through His revealed Word:

Without the Bible world evangelization is impossible. For without the Bible, we have no gospel to take to the nations, no warrant to take it to them, no idea of how to set about the task, and no hope of any success. It is the Bible that gives us the mandate, the message, the model, and the power we need for world evangelization. So let's seek to repossess it by diligent study and meditation. Let's heed its summons, grasp its message, follow its directions, and trust its power. Let's lift up our voices and make it known.[19]

NOTES:
1. David M. Howard, *The Great Commission for Today* (Downers Grove, Illinois: InterVarsity Press, 1976), page 31.
2. Martin Goldsmith, *Don't Just Stand There* (Downers Grove, Illinois: InterVarsity Press, 1976), page 8.
3. Johannes Verkuyl, "The Biblical Foundation for the Worldwide Mission Mandate," *Perspectives* (Pasadena, California: William Carey Library, 1981), page 35.
4. William Dyrness, *Let the Earth Rejoice* (Westchester, Illinois: Crossway Books, 1983), page 26.
5. John R.W. Stott, "The Bible in World Evangelization," *Perspectives* (Pasadena: William Carey Library, 1981), page 4.
6. Sam Wilson and Gordon Aeschliman, *The Hidden Half* (Monrovia, California: MARC, 1984), page 38.
7. Dyrness, page 95.
8. Dyrness, pages 115-116.
9. Dyrness, page 117.
10. Michael Griffiths, *Give Up Your Small Ambitions* (Chicago: Moody Press, 1974), page 17.
11. John R.W. Stott, *Christian Mission in the Modern World* (Downers Grove, Illinois: InterVarsity Press, 1975), page 22.
12. J. Robertson McQuilkin, *The Great Omission* (Grand Rapids: Baker Book House, 1984), pages 42-43.
13. Tom Wells, *A Vision for Missions* (Carlisle, Pennsylvania: Banner of Truth, 1985), page 123.
14. Toser, as quoted by Wells, page 35.
15. James and Marti Hefley, *Uncle Cam* (Waco, Texas: Word, Inc., 1974), page 15.
16. Clarence Hall, *Miracle on the Sepik* (Costa Mesa, California: Gift Publications, 1980), page i.
17. Ruth A. Tucker, *From Jerusalem to Irian Jaya* (Grand Rapids: Zondervan Publishing House, 1983), page 115.
18. Robert D. Foster, *The Navigator* (Colorado Springs: NavPress, 1983), page 192.
19. Stott, "The Bible in World Evangelization," page 9.

Current Events

Any vision for missions must be built on the fact that God Himself calls us to a particular world view. This is why the first building block is Scripture. God's mind is revealed in the words of Scripture. Our vision must also be relevant to the world in which we live. We must know how God's Word is integrated into the daily routines of our lives. This is why world events constitute our second building block.

SKILLS FOR BUILDING A WORLD VISION

Building a world vision through current events requires some special skills.

First, we need spiritual glasses; we need to start seeing the world the way God sees it. In Matthew 9:36, we read that Jesus had compassion on the crowds of people because they were "harassed and helpless, like sheep without a shepherd." We can safely assume that Jesus' disciples saw the same people with all of their sundry needs. However the difference between Jesus and His disciples is that He saw the people from a spiritual perspective. He saw their spiritual needs, which led to His command to His disciples to pray for the Lord of the harvest to send out workers (Matthew 9:38).

41

Second, we need "bifocal vision"[1] in order to increase our world vision through our knowledge of current events. Bifocal vision is the ability to see and care for both the world in our immediate vicinity and the bigger picture—the world we do not touch directly. Jesus was seeking to give His disciples bifocal vision when He instructed them to go to "all nations" (Matthew 28:19) and to the "ends of the earth" as well as to their hometown of Jerusalem (Acts 1:8).

Some of us err by limiting our focus to those right here at home. We think, *The needs are so great here. How can I ever think about people in India or Latin America?* Others of us prefer to avoid those near us because it is easier to care for people we do not know. Bifocal vision will help us establish a proper balance, regardless of which focus we tend to swing toward.

Third, we must be open to seeing our own sinfulness and selfishness if we are to increase our world vision through current events. Realizing the plight of people who are persecuted for their faith or seeing the horrors of starvation in the news will not only force us to pray, but will convict us about how incredibly small some of our problems really are. When we see the needs of others through the events we read about in the news, we may be challenged to stop complaining or griping about the hassles in our own lives.

Fourth, we need to remember how God works through world events if we are to build our world vision through them. Remembering how God works will further develop our perspective.

Through the ages, God has mightily used current events to direct the Church. He used historic events in the Roman Empire to direct the Church's efforts and to foster the propagation of the gospel. Even the persecution mentioned in Acts 8:1 was a God-ordained tool to help the Church fulfill the commission of Acts 1:8.

God has used the oppression of Communism in the People's Republic of China to build a strong, deeply spiritual church there. God used Mao and others to accomplish His long-term purposes. In His providence, God has allowed the church in China to undergo hostile attack, but He has used it all to His glory. James Hudson Taylor III observes what has happened in China: "Though under sustained attack, the Church in China has not just survived, it has actually flourished. From 1 million believers in 1951, when the . . . missionaries made reluctant exodus, the number of Christians in China today may have reached a staggering 50 million."[2]

An article in *National Geographic* (December 1986) on the tsetse fly of Africa records another of God's sovereign acts in the spread of the gospel. In the article, the author observes that Islam's advancement into Africa was stopped because of the fly's effect on the Muslims and their horses and camels. (The tsetse fly carries sleeping sickness.) So through a disease-inflicting fly, God preserved the people of central and southern Africa for one of the greatest revivals the Church has ever known—a revival that continues to this day.

HOW TO BUILD VISION THROUGH CURRENT EVENTS

How do we build a world vision through the knowledge of current events? We start by learning about what is happening in the world.

While a seminary student, I tried to build my world vision through a missions prayer group I attended. The participants in this group encouraged personal prayer in an assigned prayer room, so one day, I decided to try it out. I was surprised to find a copy of that day's newspaper next to a copy of the Bible and a printed prayer list in the prayer room. All I could think about was how tempted I would be to turn to the sports section or read the comics as I tried to be disciplined in prayer. To me, the newspaper was a distraction to prayer.

In an effort to find out who had "corrupted" the prayer room by putting a newspaper in it, I discovered that the newspaper was there by the instruction of the missions professor—Dr. J. Christy Wilson—who was one of the school's leading advocates of prayer. When I asked him about the newspaper, he explained, "The Bible tells us what God wants to do in the world; the newspaper tells us where He needs to do it and where we need to be involved through our prayers." From that day on, I have taken a greater interest in local and world news.

When I pick up a copy of *Time* magazine, I look to the world news first. As I do this, God directs my thinking and enlarges my vision. By reading *Time,* for example, I began to change my thinking about America's leadership in world Christianity. I read an article that said, "By the year 2000, Asia, Latin America, and Africa will have 60% of the world's Christians. . . . Protestant churches in the Third World now send out 15,000 missionaries of their own, including some to Europe and the United States."[3] This information helped me realize that churches in the Third World play a strategic role in world Christianity.

Feeding our vision for the world through current events means that we are interested in what is happening in the Middle East, that we respond in prayer when a typhoon hits Thailand, that we intercede on behalf of black and white Christians in South Africa, or that we seek to understand the dynamics of rich-versus-poor and capitalist-versus-communist struggles that occur in our world.

Feeding the vision through information on current events also means trying to gain a more Christian perspective on the news. This is why a magazine like *World Christian*[4] is so helpful. It adds God's perspective to what the secular media reports without interpreting the values or the challenges related to the issues.

Feeding our world vision does not mean that we look only to the newspaper or television news. It also means that we fully open our eyes to the possibilities and needs around us. When Jesus told His disciples, "The harvest is plentiful," (Matthew 9:37), He was telling them to open their eyes. They could see people, but He also wanted them to see their spiritual potential and needs.

We, too, need to open our eyes. The lost are all around us, so a world vision should enable us to see the folks to whom Jesus is calling us. Opening our eyes may mean noticing international influences in our own communities. While driving through Boston, for instance, I saw a Moslem mosque. In my hometown of Lexington, Massachusetts, I see an incredibly large Chinese population and an increasing Indian population. If my eyes are open, my sense of world vision can increase.

We also need to open our eyes to the vast reservoir of knowledge at our disposal. Satellite communication, telephones, and the printed page have made information about our world available in ways Christians of the past never experienced.

In our country we have no excuse for a lack of knowledge of world events. We have no reason for a narrow perspective or a shallow world vision. A mountain of knowledge is available to us that we must not take for granted or ignore.

I became much more aware of all that God has given us with respect to knowledge about our world when I visited a missionary friend in western Zambia. At noon, my friend rushed into his house to tune in the "Voice of South Africa" news on his shortwave radio. For ten minutes, he listened to a static-filled broadcast of news related to events in southern Africa. The focus was very limited, the news was far from thorough, but it was that missionary's only daily touch with the outside world. He has plenty of reasons not to know about world events, but we—who have access to news broadcasts from three networks, cable television, newspapers, and weekly news magazines—have no excuse.

WAYS TO RESPOND TO A WORLD VISION

Sometimes it is easier to stay uninformed, isn't it? The mountain of knowledge available to us can seem so steep that we do not even want to start the climb. We may look at the information available to us and respond in frustration, "There is simply too much out there to try to know about!" We need to make wise choices in response to what we learn so we can grow in our world vision without being overwhelmed by the task. Three choices seem mandatory if we are to grow in this respect.

First, we must respond in prayer. Prayer is the topic of the next building block, but we need to mention it briefly here. Prayer must be our first response to what we learn about world events because, more often than not, we are powerless to respond to world needs in any other way.

Our prayer in response to worldwide knowledge may mean active, consistent intercession for one particular geographic location or one people. It may also mean the lofting of "prayer arrows" in response to needs we hear about. A typhoon, earthquake, terrorist attack, or revolution may not be the topic of my daily prayers, but there is no reason not to respond by a single prayer at the moment I hear about a need. Perhaps my prayer will be a short, "Lord, have mercy." Perhaps I will pray for the church or Christian witness in that country. The one-time "prayer arrow" directed upward to our heavenly Father serves to remind us of *who* is in charge.

Second, we must keep from growing calloused. It is easy to hear about disasters or deaths on the news without feeling a twinge of sorrow, much less compassion for those who are suffering. Growing as world Christians, however, means that we are willing to open ourselves up to God's Spirit and ask Him to help us know how to respond to what we learn about. None of us has the emotional or spiritual capacity to respond to every need we hear about, but we must not compensate for that inability by taking on an apathetic, "who cares?" attitude. There is another realm in which we need to be softened to the Lord's influence as we learn about world news. We must not fall prey to the propaganda effect of all news reporting. When we hear a story—especially one about conflict between people, ideologies, or countries—the reporter inevitably takes sides. As Christians, we must not take sides when we approach the Lord in prayer. If we take sides, we can become hardened by hate and cannot pray for our enemies as we are commanded to do. The ayatollah, communist leaders, revolutionaries, Marxists, and anti-Christian secularists all need the Lord. If we forget that, our world view will be hampered by our biases.

Third, we must seek a manageable impact. Learning about world events can overwhelm and depress us to the point of inaction if we do not carefully focus our efforts. We must pray, entrusting all the needs we know about to the One who is all-powerful. We can also act in a faithful way, in spite of our limitations.

We may not be able to affect conflicts that we hear about regarding Libya, but there might be a Muslim student in our community whom we can invite to our home. We may not be able to stop world hunger, but we can fast for a day and send the money we would have spent on food to a hunger relief agency. (See Isaiah 58:7 on the relationship of fasting to the relief of the poor.)

We might respond to the information we accumulate by learning about a certain country or learning a foreign language. We cannot change the world single-handedly, but we can make a difference through our prayers and efforts.

World Vision, a hunger-relief organization, publishes a poster that reflects our need for a manageable impact. In one corner, there is a picture of a mass of people with the question, "How do you help one billion hungry people?" In the lower corner, there is a picture of a wide-eyed child holding his empty food bowl with the answer, "One at a time."

We increase our world vision by learning about what is happening in the world around us. We put our vision into practice by acting in response to what we have learned.

A CASE STUDY FOR BUILDING A WORLD VISION

One of the greatest challenges facing the Church in the days ahead is how to respond to urbanization. The world's population, especially in the developing world, is dramatically increasing—a fact we might not be aware of here in the United States.

David Bryant briefly outlines the impact of urbanization in the Third World:

> In 1983, 4.7 billion people inhabited the earth. By 1990, that number will rise to 5.3 billion; by the middle of the next century, we will have 9 billion inhabitants. Most of that growth will take place in the less developed world. Today, 10 out of every 11 babies born are born in the Third World. With most of the unreached currently in Africa and Asia, what will it mean to have 75% of our planet's population residing there within two decades?[5]

Bryant asks a good question, especially since most of this growth will be in cities. He goes on to say, "It's a fact that where the cities go, the nations go, and so goes the world. So, unless Christians successfully confront the major urban problems of our day, we will soon face unfathomable difficulties in preaching the gospel, and we will be up against cultural and moral forces undreamed of today."[6]

To add to our knowledge of this current phenomenon, let's consider some statistics from David Barrett's research:

- In 1986, the world's five largest cities were Tokyo/Yokohama (21.8 million), Mexico City (18.4 million), New York (18.3 million), Shanghai (17.5 million), and Sao Paolo (15 million).

- In 1987, 400 million Third World country dwellers streamed into cities.

- By 1999, Mexico City will be the world's most polluted city, with 6 million cars and a population growth rate of 1.1 million people per year.

- By 2000, the world's five largest cities are predicted to be Mexico City (27.6 million), Shanghai (25.9 million), Tokyo/Yokohama (23.8 million), Beijing (22.8 million), and Sao Paolo (21.5 million).

- By 2050, the world's five largest cities are predicted to be Shanghai (42.1 million), Mexico City (41.5 million), Beijing (36.9 million), Bombay (35 million), and Calcutta (34.4 million). Four of these five cities are presently considered to be nonChristian.

- By 2050, there will be eighty cities that Barrett calls "urban super giants"—cities with more than 10 million people.

- By the year 2400, the world is predicted to be 95 percent urbanized.[7]

Are you overwhelmed? Obviously some of these statistical predictions have a wide margin of error, but the general consensus is clear: urbanization is perhaps the greatest "current event" challenge of our time. With this challenge before us, how can we go about building a realistic world vision? I'd like you to consider the following suggestions as an example of how to respond to world events in a vision-building endeavor:

1. Choose one city as your focus. Pray for that city; learn all you can about it; start a file on it, collecting any articles you read about that city.

2. Contact a Christian ministry working in that city (if there is one), and become more familiar with that mission's work.

3. If there is no direct work in that city, try to find out which mission agencies broadcast Christian radio programs into the city.

4. Pray for and seek out an opportunity to meet someone, perhaps an international student, from that city.

5. Find out the names of political leaders in that country and city and pray for them by name.

6. Seek to understand more about urbanization and why it is happening. Read news articles about the trend toward urbanization.

7. If you can contact a Christian church or ministry in that city (or one that works indirectly to reach that city), find out about one individual for whom you can pray.

8. Consider financial involvement in a ministry or church related to that city. (For more information on this, see building block seven.)

9. Encourage others in your Christian fellowship to pray with you for that city. (This topic is covered in building block six.)

10. Pray, plan, and save so that you might be able to visit that city in the future. (For more information, see building block five.)

When we confront current events and the awesome magnitude of the world, we run the risk of shrinking away and retreating to our safe, little, manageable worlds. But building a world vision means that we learn to think small in response to the big picture we learn about. We can do our part, even if it seems insignificant, because we know that God's perspective includes His concern for every sparrow that falls to the ground (Matthew 10:29).

Malcolm Muggeridge expressed the Christian perspective succinctly. He says, "Christianity is not a statistical view of life. That there should be more joy in heaven over one sinner who repents than over all the hosts of the just, is an anti-statistical proposition."[8]

God sees our responses to the world, no matter how small they may seem. He will work through our compassionate responses to the world around us to change it. When we keep this thought in mind, our world visions will grow!

NOTES:

1. The Association of Church Missions Committees (P.O. Box ACMC, Wheaton, Illinois 60189) publishes a world Christian discipleship series entitled *Bi-focals* that concentrates on the dual growth necessary for healthy discipleship.

2. From the introduction of David Adeney, *China: The Church's Long March* (Ventura, California: Regal, 1985), page 9.

3. *Time,* December 27, 1982.

4. *World Christian* magazine is published bimonthly by World Christian, Inc., P.O. Box 5199, Chatsworth, California 91313.

5. David Bryant, *With Concerts of Prayer* (Downers Grove, Illinois: InterVarsity Press, 1984), page 108.

6. Bryant, page 109.

7. David B. Barrett, *World-Class Cities and World Evangelization* (Birmingham, Alabama: New Hope, 1986), pages 45-47.

8. Malcolm Muggeridge, *Something Beautiful for God* (New York: Harper and Row, 1971), page 28.

Prayer

If we look to Scripture, we find that God wants "all men to be saved and to come to a knowledge of the truth" (1 Timothy 2:4; see also 2 Peter 3:9). We also find that the Lord Jesus' return to earth is contingent on the fulfillment of the Great Commission: "And this gospel of the kingdom will be preached in the whole world as a testimony to all nations, and then the end will come" (Matthew 24:14). Yet when we look at the world around us we wonder, *O Lord, how shall these things be?* We feel overwhelmed, overburdened, sometimes even hopeless.

Discovering God's perspective of love and redemption from His Holy Word and becoming informed about the reality of our world's deep needs should drive us to our knees in prayer. Surely, as David Bryant points out, "God is calling us to stand in the gap (Ezekiel 22:30) primarily as a people of prayer."[1]

Jesus emphasized the importance of prayer as He taught His disciples. When Jesus saw the multitudes in need, for instance, He did not tell His disciples to go out and meet all of those needs. Instead, He told them to call on the Lord of the harvest to send out workers into the harvest (Matthew 9:36-38).

WHY IS PRAYER SO IMPORTANT?

Prayer is an essential building block in constructing our world vision because it gives us a perspective on who is in charge and it is a tool God uses to change us.

Prayer reminds us of who is in charge. In Psalm 46:10, the psalmist speaks God's Word to us: "Be still, and know that I am God; I will be exalted among the nations, I will be exalted in the earth." Note that the psalmist first says to "be still." Being quiet—still—before God in prayer is essential to knowing His perspective.

Malcolm Muggeridge describes God as being "the friend of silence."[2] He is the friend of silence because He speaks when we are quiet. When we are quiet, the Lord delivers us from our presumptuous thinking and reminds us that He is the one Sovereign Lord of the earth. One translator interprets Psalm 46:10 to mean that we need to "cease striving" (NASB) so we can see world evangelization in its proper perspective: The Almighty God is in charge; *He* will accomplish His purposes.

According to the unknown author of the prayer classic, *The Kneeling Christian,* the Devil "makes us believe that we can do more by our own efforts than by our prayer."[3] According to that author, the Devil wants to make us think this because,

> there is nothing that the devil dreads so much as prayer. His great concern is to keep us from praying. He loves to see us "up to our eyes" in work— provided we do not pray. He does not fear because we are eager and earnest Bible students—provided we are little in prayer. Someone has wisely said, "Satan laughs at our toiling, mocks at our wisdom, but trembles when we pray."[4]

Why does Satan have such a great fear of prayer? Because prayer puts us in touch with the Almighty God, the only One powerful enough to change the world. Tom Wells explains the priority of prayer in relationship to world evangelization. He says,

> Prayer is our first work in the harvest. And the reason is not hard to find. It is this: the harvest has a "Lord." He oversees the harvest. Someone supplies the workers. Someone controls the progress. And that "Someone" is God. Our first business is not to look at the size of the harvest. Our first business is to pray to our God.[5]

Yes! Our first business is to pray to God, but prayer is hard work. Praying to the Lord of the harvest implies that we trust Him with the results of the harvest. In other words, the harvest may not be exactly the way we had envisioned it.

Praying to the Lord of the harvest also implies that we believe our prayers will make a difference. Yet many of us (and I am the foremost sinner of all) act as if we do not really believe in prayer. We say we believe in the power of prayer, but our actions deny that fact. The lack of priority attention we give to prayer, the fact that we rely far too much on our own power rather than on God's, and the frenetic activity that many of us maintain reveal one truth: we have a hard time believing in the power of prayer. As a result, we face a spiritual power failure in our efforts to fulfill the Great Commission. We remember the command to go and make disciples, but forget that all authority belongs to Jesus. We forget who is really in charge.

Dr. J. Robertson McQuilkin summarizes our failure to believe in the power of prayer with a potent challenge: "Is there any wonder that the church has experienced a massive power failure so that darkness envelops the world for which we are to be lights? The connection with our power source is so tenuous, so sporadic, that we flicker and often seem simply to blink out . . . above all, we are powerless because our prayer is peripheral, a tepid formality, while God is calling us to mighty intercessory warfare."[6]

We need to pray because prayer puts us in touch with God; it leads us to the Lord of the harvest. Prayer makes us see that the harvest is His, and that we are simply His laborers. If we will be still and realize who He is, we will plug into the source of power that we need to be His witnesses.

Prayer changes us. Richard Foster writes, "To pray is to change. Prayer is the central avenue God uses to transform us."[7] When we go to the Lord of the harvest in prayer, He changes us so that we see other people and ourselves through His priorities.

When some 575 college students gathered in Toronto, Ontario, Canada, in 1946 for the first Student Missions Conference of InterVarsity Christian Fellowship (the precursor of the Urbana Missionary Conferences), the hymn that united them was Margaret Clarkson's "We Come, O Christ, To Thee." These students, many of whom later became missionaries and great Christian leaders (including Jim Elliot, David Howard, Ralph Winter, J. Christy Wilson), came together in the spirit of prayer. Their priorities were straight: to worship the Almighty God, to let Him change them, and to go out in His name. Verse five of Clarkson's hymn summarizes their vision:

> We worship Thee, Lord Christ,
> Our Savior and our King,
> To Thee our youth and strength
> Adoringly we bring:
> So fill our hearts,

That men may see Thy life in us
And turn to Thee.[8]

Yes, prayer changes us. This is the testimony of those
God has used in missions. Hudson Taylor was changed as he
prayed, and God used him mightily in China and in the
history of missions. Taylor learned through the great man of
faith, George Müller, to rely on God alone through constant
prayer. He said, "God chose me because I was weak enough.
God does not do His great works by large committees. He
trains someone to be quiet enough, and little enough, and
then He uses *him*."[9]

Prayer forced Adoniram Judson, missionary to Burma, to
greater depths of spirituality. Through Jeanne Marie Guyon's
writings, he (like Taylor) was influenced to be quiet before
God, leaving the results of his ministry in God's hands.[10]

Prayer changes us because it is, in effect, a surrendering
of ourselves to God. Prayer is a conscious recognition that we
are not in control, and that there is one to whom we look for
His will because He is infinitely wiser. In prayer we yield our
wills to God's will.

Such yielding is not easy. We like to be in control. We
struggle to allow Jesus to be our Lord. We identify with the
striving and challenge of letting go that Michael Griffiths
describes:

"Take my life"—he said,
But in the busy days ahead
Forgot and took it back again.
If "Take my life" your prayer should be,
Then make it plain,
And as a living sacrifice,
Once on the altar,
Keep it there.[11]

Prayer changes us because it unites us with God's will. It puts us at cross-purposes with the world. Theologian David Wells likens prayer to rebellion: "What, then, is the nature of petitionary prayer? It is, in essence, rebellion against the world in its fallenness, the absolute and undying refusal to accept as normal what is pervasively abnormal. It is, in this negative aspect, the refusal of every agenda, every scheme, every interpretation that is at odds with the norm as originally established by God."[12]

To pray is to change because prayer is God's method of change as He works in the spirit. To pray is to change because through prayer we surrender our will to God. To pray is to change because prayer reshapes our thinking about the world. To pray is in a sense to rebel against the corruption of sin in our world and to seek to accomplish God's purposes.

If we desire to have a growing world vision, we must faithfully pray to God.

THOSE WHO PRAY CHANGE THE WORLD

Even if we are theologically convinced that God works through prayer, it is helpful to see examples of others who have prayed. The following examples of Nehemiah, Hudson Taylor, Jim Elliot, and Christians murdered in the People's Republic of China should help motivate us to prayer!

Nehemiah. While the people of Israel were in exile, Nehemiah had a vision of God demonstrating His faithfulness to His people before their pagan captors. God placed a vision on Nehemiah's heart to rebuild the wall around the city of Jerusalem. In Nehemiah 1:4-5, Nehemiah mourns, fasts, and prays before God. He starts his prayer with the words, "O LORD, God of heaven, the great and awesome God, who keeps his covenant of love with those who love him and obey his commands."

Nehemiah knew who was in charge. He knew his vision was in vain without God's greatness on his side. He continues his prayer, reminding God of His past promises (Nehemiah's familiarity with God's Word allowed him to pray according to God's revealed will), confessing his sins and the sins of his people, and asking God to act so that He would be recognized—even in a pagan land.

God's answer to Nehemiah's prayer of faith is recorded in Nehemiah 6:16:

> When all our enemies heard about this [the completion of the wall], all the surrounding nations were afraid and lost their self-confidence, because they realized that this work had been done with the help of our God.

May God give us such success through prayer!

Hudson Taylor. God laid a spiritual burden for the great nation of China on the heart of this young man. Prayer was a central part of Taylor's life and the lives of all the missionaries he influenced to join the China Inland Mission. As Taylor studied China and the needs of each province, he faced a map and an open Bible. "Prayer was the only way by which his burdened heart could obtain any relief."[13]

Taylor's prayers and actions helped change the nature of world missions. God gave Taylor the vision to go inland, not just to approach the coastal cities. This vision influenced the founding of missions like Africa Inland Mission, Sudan Interior Mission, and others. Taylor also left behind the traditional English attire of the day, donning a Chinese robe and wearing his hair in a pigtail so he could more effectively reach the Chinese people. By so doing, Taylor became a pacesetter in cross-cultural adaptation.

Jim Elliot. Jim Elliot, one of the most famous twentieth-century missionaries, died at the hands of the Auca Indians in 1955,[14] but the impact of his life continues today.[15]

God mightily used Jim Elliot—even in his shortened life—because he was faithful in prayer, believing that the "saint who advances on his knees never retreats."[16]

> After reading, digesting, and recording, Jim set himself to praying. He had lists of people to pray for, a list for each day of the week, and if time alone in his room was limited, he prayed as he walked up to breakfast on campus, or as he stood in line in the dining hall.[17]

Elliot understood the meaning of spiritual warfare through prayer and, like Abel (Hebrews 11:4), "he still speaks, even though he is dead." Elliot prayed that God would use his life mightily; he was submitted to Him as Lord. God answered Elliot's prayer by making him a twentieth-century martyr whose life and words have stirred hundreds of others to missions commitments and deeper convictions regarding world vision.

The People's Republic of China. There is no one individual to single out in this example (although many were the spiritual children and grandchildren of Hudson Taylor), but the spiritual activity taking place in The People's Republic of China today is a testimony to God's work through prayer.

In the late forties and early fifties, hundreds of missionaries were ousted from China. Yet Carl Lawrence notes that the great awakening happening in China today has come because "those who left China on their knees never got up. They left physically but never spiritually."[18] He goes on to pay tribute to these people of prayer:

> They were not defeated; they simply continued to do battle in one of the toughest arenas of all: intercessory

prayer. They were often maligned for not realizing that this was a "different world we live in, and there is nothing you can do for China." Few were (or have been) recognized for their contribution to the building of His kingdom. They nevertheless continued hour by hour, day by day, and year by year, remembering by name those they left behind in the villages and communities that spread across China. Their work was far beyond any job description which man might design.[19]

They prayed, and God answered. Their perseverance in prayer has paid off. Their faithfulness in world-changing praying has contributed to God's great work in China, a work that only He knows in full.

LEARNING TO PRAY FOR A WORLD VISION

Prayer is a great challenge to all of us because it does not come naturally. It is a spiritual discipline or exercise that turns our attention toward God.

When we are exhorted to pray and hear examples of those who prayed faithfully, we can easily overreact. We may have been living a prayerless life, yet may attempt to imitate the great saints we have heard of by praying for four hours a day or all night long. But more often than not, a sudden burst of such zealous prayer will discourage us. When we are spiritually out of condition, a four-hour, intercessory prayer session is like trying to run a marathon without any training or while being thirty-five pounds overweight. We need to start praying where we are, in accordance with our present spiritual condition.

With this need to pray according to our spiritual condition in mind, we are free to hear the teaching that prayer is measured, "not by time, but by intensity."[20] We need to learn to think of prayer in terms like "passionate" or "fervent" rather than in terms of duration. If duration becomes our measure, we may lose our desire to pray.

We can enhance our prayer for missions if we remember to apply the following principles.

1. Start with worship. Like Nehemiah, we must recognize that in prayer we come to the Lord of Heaven and earth.

2. Confess our sins. God's purpose is to change us, and confession opens us to hear His voice.

3. Start small. If we pray for no one in missions work now, adding just one person to our prayer list is progress.

4. Pray specifically. We should choose a people group, a missionary, or a country for which we can pray rather than offering generic, "bless the missionaries," prayers.

5. Become a "prayer champion" for someone in another land or culture. One of my missionary friends, Marc Lashway, has defined three categories of people who pray: a *pray-er* is one who prays for him sporadically; a *prayer warrior* is someone who prays for him regularly (weekly or daily); a *prayer champion* is one who not only prays for him every day, but who requests prayer for him in any Christian prayer gathering—who continually champions the cause of prayer for him.

6. Use available resources to direct your prayers. Some helpful resources are the Operation Mobilization prayer cards[21] or the *Frontier Fellowship* global prayer digest.[22]

7. If you are praying for a missionary, read his or her newsletters and research the place where that missionary serves so you can pray intelligently. Few missionaries in great urban centers need prayer for protection from poisonous snakes, but they may need prayer for their protection from muggers or crazy drivers!

In his book, *Excellence in Leadership,* John White tells of one missionary who traveled to Buenos Aires, Argentina, with her luggage full of buttons, needles, and a variety of other things she thought she would need in a "backward" country. When she entered the sophisticated city of 7.5 million people, she was embarrassed at how ill-prepared she was.[23] In the same way, our prayers may be mismatched to the people we are praying for if we don't know anything about the area in which they live.

GOD WORKS THROUGH PRAYER!

Prayer, missions, and evangelism are interrelated because prayer brings us face to face with God and His plans. As Bishop Houghton says in the hymn, "Facing a task unfinished, that drives us to our knees, a need that, undiminished, rebukes our slothful ease. We, who rejoice to know thee, renew before thy throne the solemn pledge we owe thee—to go and make thee known."[24]

We must pray in order to face the unfinished task of world evangelism. We must pray if we desire to build a personal world vision. The need, the opportunity, and the Lord all drive us to our knees. And as we pray we will see the powerful ways in which God works, even ways that we do not know or understand.

Through our prayers, God allows us to be part of His changing the world. I'd like to share with you an example of how God works through prayer.

David Howard was a missionary in Colombia, South America, when God seemed to be answering many, many prayers. New believers were everywhere! God worked mightily, and David rejoiced to see this fruit. But at the same time, David's older brother, Phil, toiled away amongst the Slavey Indians in Canada's northwest territories. Phil had worked with these Indians for fourteen years without one convert.

One night, David shared his concern for his brother, Phil,

with the Indians he was working with in Colombia. After sharing his concern, David sat down. The village leader rose and invited the people to pray. David describes what happened next: "He didn't have to repeat the invitation. Two hundred people went to their knees immediately and began to pray. Their custom is for all to pray out loud together. . . . That evening they prayed for one hour and fifteen minutes without stopping. They poured out their hearts for Phil and his wife, Margaret, and for those Canadian Indians."[25]

The Colombian Indians' concern for Phil continued long after their prayer session. They sent letters of encouragement and continued to pray.

David Howard found out later that Phil, after fourteen years of ministry, had reached an all-time spiritual low. He was thinking, *What's the use?* He wondered why he should persevere. One night he went to bed defeated and discouraged, but the next morning he awoke with a new joy and courage to continue the work to which God had called him.

When the two brothers compared dates, the times coincided exactly: the very night that Phil went to bed discouraged and awoke revived was the night that the Colombian Indians had spent time in zealous prayer on his behalf. And not only Phil's spirits were revived; in a short while, the Spirit began to work, and the first converts of the Slavey Indian tribe reported their decisions to Phil. By ones and twos they started to come, in answer to the prayers of others 4,000 or more miles away!

What a privilege we have to go to God in prayer and beseech Him—not only that He will make us like His Son, Jesus Christ, but that He will work mightily in the world!

NOTES:
1. David Bryant, *With Concerts of Prayer* (Downers Grove, Illinois: InterVarsity Press, 1984), page 16.

2. Malcom Muggeridge, *Something Beautiful for God* (New York: Harper and Row, 1971), page 66.
3. Unknown author, *The Kneeling Christian* (Grand Rapids: Zondervan Publishing House, 1971), page 20.
4. *Kneeling Christian,* page 17.
5. Tom Wells, *A Vision for Missions* (Carlisle, Pennsylvania: Banner of Truth, 1985), page 138.
6. J. Robertson McQuilkin, *The Great Omission* (Grand Rapids: Baker Book House, 1984), pages 64, 67.
7. Richard J. Foster, *Celebration of Discipline* (New York: Harper and Row, 1978), page 30.
8. From *Hymns II* (Downers Grove, Illinois: InterVarsity Press, 1976), page 22. Copyright © Hope Publishing Company, Carol Stream, IL 60188. All rights reserved. Used by permission.
9. John Pollock, *Hudson Taylor and Maria* (Grand Rapids: Zondervan Publishing House, 1962), page 125.
10. Honore Willsie Morrow, *Splendor of God* (Grand Rapids: Baker Book House, 1929), page 188.
11. Michael Griffiths, *Give Up Your Small Ambitions* (Chicago: Moody Press, 1974), page 148.
12. David Wells, "Prayer: Rebelling Against the Status Quo," *Perspectives on the World Christian Movement* (Pasadena, California: William Carey Library, 1981), page 124.
13. Dr. and Mrs. Howard Taylor, *Hudson Taylor's Spiritual Secret* (Philadelphia: CIM, 1958), page 78.
14. For the account of this story see Elisabeth Elliot's *Through Gates of Splendor.*
15. Many have been motivated to a deeper walk with the Lord through the journals of Jim Elliot as they are recorded in Elisabeth Elliot's book, *Shadow of the Almighty.*
16. Elisabeth Elliot, *Shadow of the Almighty* (Grand Rapids: Zondervan Publishing House, 1958), page 53.
17. Elliot, *Shadow of the Almighty,* page 52.
18. Carl Lawrence, *The Church in China* (Minneapolis: Bethany House Publishers, 1985), page 117.
19. Lawrence.
20. *Kneeling Christian,* page 77.
21. Operation Mobilization prayer cards have pertinent information and prayer requests for seventy spiritually needy nations. They are available from STL Books, P.O. Box 28, Waynesboro, Georgia 30830.
22. The *Frontier Fellowship* global prayer digest is published monthly by the U.S. Center for World Mission, 1605 East Elizabeth, Pasadena, California 91104.
23. John White, *Excellence in Leadership* (Downers Grove, Illinois: InterVarsity Press, 1986), pages 41-42.
24. *Hymns II,* page 174.
25. This story is told in total in David Howard's *The Great Commission for Today* (Downers Grove, Illinois: InterVarsity Press, 1976), pages 98-102.

Reading

How did William Carey, the man considered to be the "father" of the modern missionary movement, get his vision for world missions? From Scripture? From prayer? From current events?

I am sure all of these building blocks played a part in his life, but his initial spark of interest in missions and concern for those beyond the reach of the gospel came from reading. According to missions biographer Ruth Tucker, Carey's missions zeal was ignited by reading *Captain Cook's Voyages.* God used accounts of the explorer's efforts in the South Pacific to stir Carey to see the Scriptures and the world in a new light.[1]

In the same way, reading can build our missions zeal and world vision. We can be informed by reading publications like *National Geographic,* or news-oriented publications. We can turn to many Christian resources for biographical histories (like *From Jerusalem to Irian Jaya*) or for current developments in missions (such as those available through the Evangelical Missions Information Service[2]). By digging into the vast array of published material available to us, we can use the information boom to our advantage and to benefit the people we are trying to reach for the Lord.

READING TO HELP BUILD A WORLD VISION
If we go to a local Christian bookstore, we may not find much material on missions. Although some bookstore owners are very missions oriented, most missions books do not sell as well as books on other subjects. Therefore, our search for missions books may begin with some frustration. On the other hand, if we write to publishers that specialize in missions books, like the William Carey Library[3] or MARC (the Missions Advanced Research and Communication Center),[4] we may find that the deluge of missions works available overwhelms us.

So where do we start? Generally, it is good to read broadly at the beginning. Look over the available resources you know about (including those in this book's bibliography) and choose a sampling from the various categories. If we read material from the five general categories listed below, we can achieve a good balance of growth in our missions-related reading.

1. Missions Histories. In Psalm 105:5, the psalmist writes, "Remember the wonders he has done, his miracles, and the judgments he pronounced." The psalmist writes these words to the "descendants of Abraham" (verse 6) to urge them to have faith in God.

We, too, need to remember God's past works so we can believe Him to do great things in the present and the future. We need to remember God's past work so we do not repeat the same mistakes our spiritual forefathers made. Remembering the past also helps us realize that God has been at work since Creation. We are not into something new; God has sovereignly been at work through the ages.

Missions histories can be very boring. But there is hope. First, there is hope because writers are making a greater effort to make church and missions history come alive. The aforementioned work by Ruth Tucker, *From Jerusalem to Irian*

Jaya, is perhaps the best, recent effort in this respect. Second, there is hope because the missions histories are only part of our reading diet. Nevertheless, they must be a part of our reading if we are to understand God's work in the past.

Some missions history must be a part of our reading. The history of the church in China might fascinate us, but an overall history of the Church (like the seven-volume set by Kenneth Scott Latourette, *A History of the Expansion of Christianity*[5]) may intimidate us. So it may be best to start with abbreviated histories like some of the articles in *Perspectives on the World Christian Movement.*[6] Without a sense of history, we can erroneously think that missions is something totally new in the Church. Our reading of Scripture plus missions histories should help dispel that notion.

2. Biographies. God gives us the witness of His faithful servants in the past to encourage us to be faithful in the present. In Hebrews 11:1-12:1, the writer lists a great "cloud of witnesses" in an effort to encourage the persecuted believers to "run with perseverance the race marked out for us."

William Carey, Adoniram Judson, Hudson Taylor, Cameron Townsend, and Jim Elliot are all missionaries whose lives we should know about. C.T. Studd, Mary Slessor, John and Betty Stam, or David Livingstone are certainly part of the great "cloud of witnesses" God has given us to inspire our faithfulness in ministry and missions vision. If we are to grow in our world vision, we need to know about the people God has used in the past. Biographies give us a personal encounter with those we could otherwise never meet. Biographies enable us to be inspired and challenged by the lives of those who have gone before us.

3. Current Issues in Missions. When the church in Antioch commissioned Saul and Barnabas as its first missionaries, it was probably not big news in that city. As a matter of fact, the local media probably did not even notice. But that event launched a worldwide ministry that continues 2,000 years later. So it was a great event from the perspective of Heaven's news bureau.

The fact that developments in the Church often escape the notice of the secular press makes it mandatory for us to supplementour study of current events with reading on current issues and events in missions. We must look to other believers to help us interpret the events of our time. This may mean we look deeper into world events by reading books on the subject that are written from a Christian perspective. Contemporary examples of such reading might include a Christian's perspective on South Africa (like Gordon Aeschliman's *Apartheid: Crisis in Black and White*) or a Christian's report of life in Communist countries (like David Ziomek's *A Christian View of Russia*).

Reading on current events in missions might also mean reading about events, like the sending of Saul and Barnabas in Acts 13, that our world does not know about. Learning about Wycliffe's work with some obscure tribe in south Asia will not usually come from reading *Time* or *Newsweek*. To find out about these current events, we need to read missionary periodicals and newsletters from people on the mission field. We may also need to pursue some lesser known books so we can see how God works in our world.

4. Cross-Cultural Understanding. We can learn much by reading some of the more technical publications related to missions work. Our understanding of what it means to communicate the gospel across cultures can be built by reading books like *Christianity Confronts Culture* or *The Making of a Missionary*.

Reading about what it really means to adapt to another culture or learn a new language can help us as we pray for missionaries or interact with internationals in our neighborhoods.

For most of us, our reading time is limited, and we do well to read a missions history, a few biographies, or a book on a current missions issue during the course of a year. But our missions vision "diet" will be enriched if we read a book on cultural anthropology or cross-cultural understanding. Such material will help us understand the more technical side of world evangelization.

5. *General Missions Resources.* The Association of Church Missions Committees and *World Christian* magazine offer resources that can be used personally or in an effort to build the missions vision of others. Many mission organizations also publish materials to help stimulate missions awareness on the local church level or in one-on-one discipling relationships.

Other not-so-direct missions resources might be books designed to stimulate deeper commitment to the Christian life. Some of the classics, like A.W. Tozer's *Pursuit of God* and *The Knowledge of the Holy* and E.M. Bounds' books on prayer, are not missions-oriented *per se,* but exhort us in areas that build the foundation of discipleship on which missions rests.

SET REALISTIC GOALS FOR READING

Confronting the array of missions resources can overwhelm us if we do not have a more defined target. Setting goals to accomplish balanced missions reading can help us see progress and can guide us toward a proper balance of vision-building intake.

One way to make missions reading manageable would be to set a goal regarding the quantity of books or pages to be read. A one-year personal goal sheet might look like this:

1. To read one missions history on the current age of missions, 1700 to the present.

2. To read three missions biographies: two of them about people in the past and one about a person who lived in the twentieth century.
3. To read one book related to the rich-poor struggle and how it affects missionary work.
4. To read the preparatory information used by a mission that we are familiar with in order to understand what preparation is required of missionaries who work in a new culture.
5. To read one specific resource book on the biblical basis for missions.

With these goals in mind, we could go to a bookstore, speak to a missionary, or write to a missions professor or organization and request reading recommendations in the areas in which we desire to grow.

Another way to make missions reading more manageable would be to adopt a goal motto. One of the goals I have set for myself on various occasions is to know "something about everywhere and everything about somewhere."

With this motto as my goal, I have set out to learn the names and locations of every country in the world, which isn't as hard as you might think, and to know the name of each country's capital and the country's major religions. This is an example of my effort to know "something about everywhere."

It's a little more challenging to learn "everything about somewhere." There are more resources available if I choose to learn everything about China, or Kenya, or Brazil than if I choose to learn about North Korea or Burkina Faso. Ideally, learning "everything about somewhere" would mean reading a biography about a missionary who worked in that country, reading a history of Christianity in that country, and finding out about the challenges missionaries (if there are any) and Christians in that country face. I would also read materials published by missions agencies that seek to reach the people of that country so I could understand the cultural and spiritual situation as well.

I know that we can never fully achieve the goal of learning "something about everywhere and everything about somewhere." However, such a goal enables me to be more zealous about God's work in the world and to learn all I can about it.

THE RESULTS OF READING TO BUILD OUR WORLD VISION

Reading missions biographies or getting involved in a missions issue helps me grow. It opens my mind and feeds me intellectually. In the process of becoming an active reader in order to build a world vision, I have found that God can use published material to teach us in at least seven ways.

1. We are inspired. When we read the biography of Henry Martyn (*My Love Must Wait*) and consider his example— he literally "burned out for God"—we are challenged!

> Refusing to live for himself, he was glad to be spent for his Saviour. He combined the convictions of an evangelical Christian, the mind of a brilliant scholar, and an almost monastic self-discipline. He was thirty-one years old when he died.[7]

The "great cloud of witnesses" that we can learn about through missionary biographies and histories inspires us to a deeper commitment in our walk with the Lord. In effect, these Christians disciple us through their example.

In his book, *Restoring Your Spiritual Passion,* Gordon MacDonald speaks to the issue of being discipled by the great saints of the past. He refers to conversations with his wife, Gail, when she noted that her sponsors (older, discipling mentors) "tend to be dead people. I have found them in the great biographies where I was able to discover the strengths of great men and women of God."[8]

I have found great inspiration in reading about David Livingstone's love for Africa. His great love for Africa caused the people to bury his heart in the center of that continent (which he had opened to the rest of the world). Livingstone loved Africa and would not leave it, even when he was very sick. He died on his knees, in the posture of prayer.[9]

Men like Cameron Townsend and George Müller are sources of inspiration for perseverance. When I read that Cameron Townsend, even in his late seventies, was awake every day "by 6:30 a.m. . . . reading the Bible, praying around the world, planning, figuring,"[10] I am encouraged to be faithful in my walk with the Lord. When I study the life of George Müller, I am convicted about my own laziness in serving the Lord. Müller, an incredible man of faith and vision, never retired. At age seventy, he recommitted himself to the task of world missions. His biographer writes,

> On March 26, 1875, he began a series of seventeen missionary tours that would take him to forty-two nations, covering two hundred thousand miles by land and water. He preached many thousands of times, and from his own estimate during these tours, he spoke to three million people.[11]

And Müller did all this between age seventy and eighty-seven, when he died!

Norman Grubb begins his biography of C.T. Studd, the great missionary pioneer, with this poem:

> He climbed the steep ascent of heaven
> Through peril, toil, and pain;

O God, to us may grace be given
To follow in his train.[12]

Reading the biographies of missionaries and histories of missions increases our world vision because they stir us to imitate the people who have gone before us.

2. *We learn from the mistakes of others.* We've all heard the saying, "Those who do not learn from the mistakes of the past are condemned to repeat them." I have discovered that reading about missions, especially reading biographies of missionaries and histories of missions, helps me learn from others' mistakes.

Adoniram Judson, David Brainerd, and Hudson Taylor had bouts with depression and melancholy. Through their lives we see that depression is a powerful tool the Devil uses to discourage people in "frontline" evangelism. From their experience we can learn to identify our own times of depression and avoid making important decisions while we are depressed that we may need to reverse later. Some missionary pioneers were gruff individuals who seemed to alienate some people while they won others. From their example we can learn to be more gentle with the people we work with.

Bob Pierce, the visionary founder of World Vision International, lived a life of great victory and great tragedy. Tremendous progress overseas was combined with marital and family trauma at home. From Bob Pierce we learn that, in the words of his daughter,

> The story of greatness is not the story of a man or woman or family who runs and never stumbles or falls; rather, it is the story of those who dare to run *and* stumble *and* fall, and who by the grace of God pick themselves up again and again and again. The story of victory is not one without pain or sacrifice or disap-

pointment, but one of holding on, of standing fast on the promises of God's Word, of knowing that while we may never understand the "whys" someday we shall see Him face to face, and it will be worth it all![13]

3. We grow in our vision of God. Many of us struggle to identify with the God of the Bible because we see in Scripture a power that we do not seem to experience in our own lives. Reading about missions, however, helps us see God's power at work, which gives us a bigger view of what God wants to do in our lives.

In his book, *On the Crest of the Wave,* Peter Wagner reports on the Holy Spirit's current movement in missions. He recounts many reports of God at work in mighty ways. One such story reveals God's power at work in the face of political and religious persecution:

In Awasa, one of the provincial capitals of southern Ethiopia, a church leader had been arrested by the Communist police. He was interrogated and punished. Then the Communist official said, "Curse the enemies of the revolution, and I will let you go." The Christian leader knew that as he said it he would be expected to raise his left fist in the Communist salute.

"I cannot do it," he responded. "Jesus told us to bless our enemies, not to curse them."

"Then you will grasp this high tension wire!" the Communist said. A bare electrical wire was held in front of him.

The Christian leader said, "In the name of Jesus!" and grabbed the wire with his bare hand. At once the whole town went into a blackout! The man was unhurt. Instead of his left fist, he raised both hands, smiled at the Communist and said, "Praise the Lord!"[14]

Missions reports like this can serve to remind us that our God is the same God who divided the Red Sea, performed miracles, and raised our Lord Jesus Christ from the dead! This God of power is our personal God. We need to be continually reminded of His greatness so that our view of Him will increase.

4. We see the people God uses. The great missionary statesman and pastor of the People's Church in Toronto, Oswald J. Smith, wrote a book entitled, *The Man God Uses.* We all want to know what kind of person God uses. We want to know whether He works only through spiritual giants or works through average people, too.

Reading to enlarge our world vision will show us that God uses average people, just like you and me! He uses imperfect sinners to do His will. He does not wait for people to become "saints" before He uses them, and He does not look for the greatest people. Instead, our reading about missions will confirm His promise that He will use the person who is "humble and contrite in spirit, and trembles at my word" (Isaiah 66:2).

William Carey was such a man. In his lifetime of missions service in India, Carey's translation and printing work "rendered the Bible accessible to more than three hundred million people."[15]

When he died, after more than forty years of ministry in India, he had translated the Bible into three major Indian languages, had founded what has become the largest newspaper in India, had established the strong and effective Baptist Church Union in India, had founded what has become the largest seminary in India, and had done more than any individual to bring the message of the Gospel of Christ to that subcontinent. *He was one simple cobbler who took God at His word, and his obedience immeasurably affected an entire subcontinent.*[16] (emphasis added)

Kenneth Strachan, the founder of the Latin America Mission and great missionary leader of our century, was a simple man who God used. From his childhood dreams of settling "in New England with the Pilgrim Fathers," and driving the Indians off with the *Deerslayer* and the rest of Fenimore Cooper's heroes,[17] Strachan grew to be a man God mightily used to bring the gospel to many people (including South American Indians!) of Latin America.

Reading about people God has used to be world-changers in the past reminds us that He wants to use us, too. Even the New Testament writers used the past heroes of faith to remind their readers that God uses ordinary people. James writes, "Elijah was a man just like us" (James 5:17), and shows how God used him in a powerful way.

5. *We grow in our ability to influence others for world evangelization.* Not every great missionary leader of the past has actually gone out in missionary service. Dawson Trotman of The Navigators, Bob Pierce of World Vision, Oswald J. Smith of the People's Church of Toronto, Harold Ockenga of Park Street Church, and the great A.J. Gordon were leaders who influenced others to go into world missions.

One of the reasons these people were used by God was that they knew of God's missions work through the ages. In one particularly powerful sermon on the need for pioneering work in missions, for instance, Oswald J. Smith drew illustrations from the lives of Paul the apostle, Robert Moffatt, David Livingstone, Dan Crawford, and David Brainerd.[18] Smith knew missions and used that knowledge to build a church that has sent dozens of people and millions of dollars into missions work around the world.

God may use missions and world vision reading to push

some of us into direct missions service, but He will also use us (as our missions vision increases) to influence others to go into missions service.

6. *We will pray for our missionaries more effectively.* One purpose of reading missions biographies, and reading about current events in missions and literature about cross-cultural adaptation, is to help us more accurately understand what people in missions settings experience. If we understand their situations, we will be better able to pray for our missionary friends and to write to them in encouraging ways. Understanding the painstaking task of Bible translation will help us be more patient with missionaries who return home with few immediate results in their ministries. Reading about the trauma of cultural adaptation will help us identify with and pray for those who serve internationally.

7. *We will see how God brings good out of adversity.* In my recent reading about apartheid, I came across the story of Caesar Molebatsi, a black, South African, Christian leader who God is using mightily.

One of his legs is wooden, a daily reminder to Caesar of the ills of South Africa. Hit by a white driver, Caesar had to listen incredulously to the judge who sympathized with the driver's need to hit a black pedestrian instead of the curb—the curb would have damaged his car. And besides, Caesar was no doubt in a white area without "due cause."

An embittered teenager, crippled for life and with a self-esteem a little lower than a car fender, Caesar decided to kill the driver, knowing that it would mean the death penalty for him. He watched the driver's daily patterns, and one day, confident of his kill, a gun in his jacket, he went to settle the score. The only hitch was that on the way, he met one of those obnox-

ious street-witnessing Christians who lacked sophisticated skills in evangelism. Asked the simple question,
"What will happen to you if you die tonight?" Caesar
instead settled his score with God, and has been working for Him ever since.[19]

Out of the pain, injustice, and hatred of that situation,
God brought a man to faith who is powerfully at work in
Christian leadership in his country. God is at work, taking
bleak situations and turning them to His good. We not only
see this pattern of God at work today, but see it in the
scriptural examples of Joseph and Saul (who became Paul).
With this pattern in mind, we, too, can look to Him to bring
good out of adversity.

GET STARTED!

The reading resources are many and the growth in missions
and world vision is almost unlimited, but we must start
somewhere. God can use a biography, an historical account,
or a missions training manual to build our vision for and
commitment to His work in the world. When we are inspired
and motivated by modern-day accounts of faith like those
seen in Hebrews 11, we will sing Frederick Faber's words
with meaning:

> Faith of our fathers! Living still:
> In spite of dungeon, fire and sword.
> O how our hearts beat high with joy
> Whenever we hear that glorious word!
> Faith of our fathers! holy faith!
> We will be true to thee till death![20]

Perhaps God will use us in equally mighty ways!

NOTES:
1. Ruth A. Tucker, *From Jerusalem to Irian Jaya* (Grand Rapids: Zondervan Publishing House, 1983), page 115.
2. For information on the publications of the Evangelical Missions Information Service, write to EMIS, P.O. Box 794, Wheaton, Illinois 60189.
3. The William Carey Library publishes a book list that can be obtained by writing to them at P.O. Box 40129, Pasadena, California 91104.
4. MARC Publications are produced by World Vision International, 919 West Huntington Drive, Monrovia, California 91016.
5. Kenneth Scott Latourette, *A History of the Expansion of Christianity* (Grand Rapids: Zondervan Publishing House, 1970). The last four volumes cover the advancement of Christianity through Protestant missions since the time of William Carey (ca. 1790).
6. Ralph Winter and Steven Hawthorne, *Perspectives on the World Christian Movement* (Pasadena, California: William Carey Library, 1981). This volume has short, six-to ten-page articles on subjects related to missions history.
7. David Bentley-Taylor, *My Love Must Wait* (Downers Grove, Illinois: Inter-Varsity Press, 1975), page 157.
8. Gordon MacDonald, *Restoring Your Spiritual Passion* (Nashville: Thomas Nelson Publishers, 1986), page 183.
9. *Classics of Christian Missions* (Nashville: Broadman Press, 1979), page 189.
10. James and Marti Hefley, *Uncle Cam* (Waco, Texas: Word, Inc., 1974), page 242.
11. Basil Miller, *George Mueller: Man of Faith and Miracles* (Minneapolis: Bethany House Publishers, 1941), page 91.
12. On the title page of Norman P. Grubb's *C.T. Studd: Cricketeer and Pioneer* (Fort Washington, Pennsylvania: Christian Literature Crusade, 1985).
13. Marilee Pierce Dunker, *Man of Vision, Woman of Prayer* (Nashville: Thomas Nelson Publishers, 1980), page 239. Copyright 1984 by The Zondervan Corporation. Used by permission.
14. Peter Wagner, *On the Crest of the Wave* (Ventura, California: Regal Books, 1983), page 140.
15. Tom Wells, *A Vision for Missions* (Carlisle, Pennsylvania: Banner of Truth, 1985), page 12.
16. Ted W. Engstrom, *Motivation to Last a Lifetime* (Grand Rapids: Zondervan Publishing House, 1984), page 30.
17. Elisabeth Elliot, *Who Shall Ascend?* (New York: Harper and Row, 1968), page 5.
18. Oswald J. Smith, *The Challenge of Missions* (Bromley, England: STL Books, 1959), page 108.
19. Gordon Aeschliman, *Apartheid: Tragedy in Black and White* (Ventura, California: Regal Books, 1986), page 16.
20. Frederick W. Faber, "Faith of Our Fathers," *Inspiring Hymns* (Grand Rapids: Singspiration, 1951), page 324.

Firsthand Experience

When we read Jesus' command in Matthew 28:19 in English, we lose some of the full impact of the phrase we translate as, "all the *nations.*" In English, this phrase sounds international and intriguing, but in reality, Jesus' command strikes at one of our most basic flaws—what sociologists call *ethnocentricity.*

Jesus commanded His disciples to go to all the *ethné,* meaning all ethnic groups. This is a challenging command because we are instinctively ethnocentric. We think that our particular ethnic group is better, superior, or more desirable than another. In our sinfulness, we think of our *ethné* as central. In contrast, our Lord commands us to go beyond our own group to all the *ethné*—to the ends of the earth.

A healthy and growing world vision requires that we grow beyond ethnocentricity, and one of the best growth inducers is to experience life beyond our normal realm. We need firsthand experience in other cultures and with other ethnic groups to grow beyond our racism, false stereotypes, and narrow world views.

Firsthand experience also gives us personal exposure to the needs of others. Franklin Graham, director of Samaritan's Purse and author of one of the biographies of Bob Pierce, reflects this truth when he writes, "How else can we get a *feel,* a realization of the need *ourselves* . . . unless we go to a mission field and experience the need firsthand?"[1]

Although a trip to the mission field may not be possible for all of us, we can pursue some options to expose ourselves to excellent, firsthand, cross-cultural experience.

A FEW EASY, CROSS-CULTURAL EXERCISES

One way to expand our world vision through cross-cultural experiences might be to eat dinner at an international restaurant or at least eat an international meal at home. Because of our cultural biases, we easily make false assumptions about others. Some of these false assumptions can be dispelled by doing something as simple as eating an international meal.

For example, the next time you eat at a Chinese restaurant, why not use the chopsticks instead of the fork?

"The chopsticks are so clumsy," you might say in protest. True, they might be clumsy for us, but our generalization that chopsticks are clumsy is quite false. The chopsticks are not clumsy; we are. For more than one billion people on earth, chopsticks are quite useful, so the problem is not in the chopsticks.

Perhaps we have an aversion to Mexican food because we think it's too hot and that it will upset us. Again, assuming that all Mexican food is hot is a false generalization. Not all Mexican food is hot; some is pretty average, and some is quite bland.

You might wonder what eating international foods has to do with missions, and I have a good answer for you. By eating international foods, we participate in an exercise that broadens our horizons; we identify with a different people group or culture. We, for even one meal, become like them, which is a basic aspect of good missionary vision.

Another simple suggestion for firsthand experience is to

visit a different area of our town or city. Visiting a Spanish-speaking area or a Chinese neighborhood reminds us that our corner of the world is not the only world. When we visit a different area, we see a new culture, hear a new language, and see people who may not look much like us. We broaden our vision when we go beyond ourselves and identify with someone else.

One of the best experiences I remember with respect to visiting an ethnically different area occurred with a small group from our youth ministry. We went into Boston to enlarge our visions.

The missionary who went with us had come from the suburbs, just like us, so he knew the stereotypes that filled our heads as we saw row houses, vacant lots, and the people of the city. Knowing the false impressions we had in mind, the missionary gave us the first assignment of our mission.

He gave us paper and pens and told us we had two hours to walk about the city. He instructed us to list all the things we observed in the city that were different from our living situation and encouraged us to focus on aspects of the city that were better than where we lived in the suburbs.

At first, the students (and leaders, too) thought, *This won't take long!* To our surprise, we observed many positive things about the city. Students came back with long lists of observations like:

> "In the city, people sit on their steps and talk to their neighbors; where I live, people are too busy to talk to their neighbors (if they even know their neighbors!)."
> "In the city, many people speak two or even more languages; I can only speak English."
> "In the city, people don't have to worry about mowing their lawns."

"In the city, the stores are much closer; you can live pretty happily without a car."

"In the neighborhood we went to, the neighbors all seemed to know each other. They told us that they protected each other. There was a sense of security and 'family' in their neighborhood, unlike mine."

"It wasn't like I pictured. I expected to see hookers and drug pushers all over the place. I am sure that they were there, but most of the people I met seemed pretty average, just like me."

A visit to a new ethnic group or an area that is culturally different from what we are accustomed to can effectively change us. Such an experience helps us to dispel our stereotypes and leads us to a more accurate understanding of others.

A third simple, but effective, way to get firsthand, cross-cultural experience is to be involved with internationals who live in our communities. There are thousands of refugees in our country to whom we can reach out with Christ's love in an effort to understand them, their culture, and their needs.[2] In addition to refugees, literally thousands of international students live and study in our country. Reaching out to the "world that has come to us"[3] can help us broaden our world perspective:

Never in the history of the Christian church has a generation of Christians had a greater opportunity to reach the nations of the world than we have in America today. . . . The frontiers of foreign missions are no longer only in Tibet, Saudi Arabia, Mongolia, and China. They are also in Boston, New York, Chicago, and Los Angeles, for they have come to the United States in the form of international visitors.[4]

Broadening our world vision can go hand-in-hand with outreach as we invite internationals into our home. My friend Norm has reached out to an Indian family he works with. When he invited them into his home, he found out that his was the first American home they had been invited into after living in the United States for five years! Through his friendship with this family, Norm has learned about India, Hinduism, and Indian culture. The Indian family has started to learn about Christ's love.

My wife, Christie, works at a hospital where there are dozens of international workers. Through simple questioning and a genuine interest in her coworkers' answers, she has increased her knowledge about Puerto Rico, China, Hong Kong, and Zimbabwe.

The world has come to us, and we are the losers if we do not take advantage of the learning opportunities God has placed before us.

A final simple way to gain cross-cultural experience and understanding is to join in worship with Christians from other ethnic groups or cultures. When we do this, our world vision expands and we realize that

God is not worshiped in any one, correct way;
God is worshiped in many languages;
the Church of Jesus Christ goes around the world;
various cultures change the style of worship, singing,
and praying, but we worship the same God.

While a college student, I started praying for the great nation of the People's Republic of China, which was, at that time, closed. About a year later, I attended a Chinese church service in a nearby community. As the people sang hymns, prayed, and preached in their Chinese dialect, I could not understand a thing, but God used that service to build my faith to pray for China. In that congregation I saw and heard a reflection of the country for which I was praying.

MORE SACRIFICIAL CROSS-CULTURAL EXPERIENCES

Firsthand cross-cultural experience does not have to be expensive, but as our vision increases and our hunger to understand other people and cultures intensifies, we may want to make sacrifices to continue our vision-building process.

Some families have chosen to invite a foreign student to live with them. This is costly in terms of time (and sometimes money), but the rewards are great. In such a situation, cultural understanding has greater opportunity to increase because the daily affairs of life make cultural differences much more evident.

Hosting an international student also allows us more opportunity to share Christ's love, which is especially exciting if the student comes from a country where missionaries are not allowed. By being a host, we can be God's agents to bring the gospel to a student who, in turn, could take it back to his or her own country.

Another way to gain cross-cultural experience is to house immigrants as they settle in this country. In light of the fact that immigrants come into our country in droves—52,000 southeast Asians in 1984 alone[5]—our opportunities to learn about other cultures while we serve these newcomers in Christ's name are endless.

My friends Roger and Marcy have undertaken this challenge for the past six years. They have shared their home with families from Cambodia, Laos, East Germany, and other locations. Their children are growing up with a firsthand knowledge of the world, and the whole family is helping others gain world visions. The cost is high, but the rewards are great.

A third, more involved way to gain cross-cultural experience, is to learn another language, especially if we can learn it from someone from another country. Learning a language and learning about a culture go hand-in-hand, enabling us to understand more about the world in which we live. The most intense and fulfilling way to gain a deeper knowledge of another culture is to travel to another country. Although it might be costly, travel is the best way to immerse oneself in another land. Personal and cultural biases are often destroyed through firsthand experience.

In the early 1800s, when Adoniram Judson (the first missionary to sail from the shores of the United States) went to Burma, a short visit to the mission field was not possible. It took Judson four months to get from Salem, Massachusetts, to Calcutta, India, so taking a two-week "vacation with a purpose" was not an option. Today we do have the option of visiting the mission field.

Traveling to other cultures has changed my life and repeatedly renewed my missions enthusiasm. Visits to Africa, Latin America, the Caribbean, and Europe have helped me see how different this world is. These visits have also helped me see the gospel's transcultural nature; Jesus Christ our Savior crosses all cultural and ethnic barriers.

Traveling has also helped me challenge others to travel, and I have seen a similar vision-expanding impact on their lives. By traveling to see other cultures and countries firsthand, these friends have returned home with a larger world view and a more vibrant vision for missions.

MAKING THE MOST OF CROSS-CULTURAL EXPERIENCE

All of these observations about cross-cultural experience might indicate that growth in world vision is guaranteed. In reality, this is far from true. Some people go to the city and, through selective observation, merely confirm their biased stereotypes. Others travel overseas and return home thinking that the rest of the world is backward or ugly. Their experience seems to cause their world vision to shrink rather than grow. So if we want to make the most of cross-cultural experiences, we must make certain decisions that will allow us to grow.

We must be willing to identify our own biases. One of the greatest dangers of prejudice is that those affected by it do not realize that they are; they simply think that their viewpoints are correct. However, if we are going to grow through experiences in other cultures, we must be willing to recognize our narrow-sightedness.

One example of our prejudicial narrow-sightedness might be the illustration I used of chopsticks in a Chinese restaurant; our bias results from our effort to explain why we cannot use chopsticks. Another example might be the observation many Americans make that "people in England drive on the *wrong* side of the road." Such a statement reveals our bias; there is nothing wrong with driving on the left. As a matter of fact, driving on the *right* in England could be fatal.

We all have our own cultural understanding about the way things ought to be; this is quite normal. But until we begin to understand that things can be different without being right or wrong, our cross-cultural learning will be hampered.

A failure to identify cultural or racial biases has been one of the greatest failures in cross-cultural work of the past. It is detrimental to attach Western culture to the gospel. Some who might have responded to the Jesus of Scripture have turned away from a culturally-attached Jesus.

E. Stanley Jones, the great missionary to India, lamented this failure to separate Western culture from the gospel in his comment regarding Gandhi's rejection of Christianity:

"Racialism has many sins to bear, but perhaps its worst sin was the obscuring of Christ in an hour when one of the greatest souls born of a woman was making his decision."[6]

To avoid such "obscuring," we must be sure to present Christ, rather than our culture, to the people we seek to touch.

We must become world Christians, not just well-traveled Americans. Traveling to a variety of locations around the world and seeing other American travelers has helped me understand the phrase "ugly American" in a new way. The American traveler often acts as though foreigners are his servants, that any inconvenience is intolerable, that beggars and lame people on the street are there to be photographed, and that other countries are subservient to or are a subsidiary of the United States.

As followers of Jesus Christ, however, we should be characterized by graciousness toward all people. As those who consider humility to be a high virtue, Christians should act humbly when visiting another church or neighborhood— no matter how different it is from what we are accustomed to.

One term that describes people who are attuned to or experienced in international cultures is "citizens of the world." As Christians, we should be more than world citizens, for we are citizens of another world; we are citizens of Christ's Kingdom. As such, we are only visitors on this earth who are called to display Christ's character in whatever culture, ethnic environment, or country we are in.

We must ask questions and listen. When I prepare to go into another culture, I write out a list of questions that I hope to ask of fellow Christians, and anyone else with whom I can strike up a conversation.

Asking good questions requires a little preparation— like reading something about that culture or ethnic group— and then asking questions in a way that communicates our interest and desire to learn. If we ask questions only to sound intelligent, and do not carefully listen to our cross-cultural friends' responses, we show that we are more interested in hearing ourselves talk than in learning. An old sage once said, "With two ears and one mouth, I ought to be listening twice as much as I talk." This is good advice if we are to learn from people of other cultures. *We must be willing to change.* When Hudson Taylor returned to England, he discovered that his experiences in China had changed him. His biographer, John Pollock, records an experience by which Taylor realized that his outlook had been transformed by his time in China:

> As the full congregation rose to sing the last hymn, Taylor looked around. Pew upon pew of the prosperous, bearded merchants, shopkeepers, visitors; demure wives in their bonnets and crinolines, scrubbed children trained to hide their impatience; the atmosphere of smug piety sickened him. He seized his hat and left. "Unable to bear the sight of a congregation of a thousand or more Christian people rejoicing in their own security, while millions are perishing for lack of knowledge, I wandered out on the sands alone in great spiritual agony."[7]

Hudson Taylor's experiences overseas made it difficult for him to accept the inequities of the two worlds in which he had lived. Anyone who has traveled to Mexico City, Calcutta, or virtually any developing world location knows the same feeling. How dare we complain when we have so much? How can such inequities exist?

Beware. Firsthand experiences in another culture, ethnic group, or country are life changing. One woman told me that her trip to South America made her stop window-shopping. She learned that she had so much in comparison to the people she met in South America, and said, "If I go window-shopping, it makes me think I need more."

Firsthand experience in another culture may increase our perspective of God, who is worshiped in a myriad of ways in a variety of languages. Firsthand experiences may break down our stereotypes, causing us to discard our narrow-sighted attitudes. Firsthand experiences will also change our insights into needs and priorities.

For instance, after visiting with a pastor friend, my wife and I drove home disturbed. The pastor had told us about his personal and ministry priorities—all of which were quite acceptable by North American standards—but made no mention of those who hurt. He demonstrated no compassion for those in the Third World; he manifested no concern for missions. As we thought about our time with our pastor friend, I remembered an experience my wife and I shared in Zambia. "He has never held a starving child," I explained, and in that statement my wife and I realized that our vision, priorities, and even personal standards of what was "acceptable" had been changed because of our firsthand experience in another culture.

It is frightening to have our stereotypes broken down and our worlds enlarged. Such growth causes us to leave the security of our narrower definitions. Yet God wants us to grow; indeed, if we are unwilling to grow, we will die. Mary Slessor, missionary to West Africa, stated, "Courage is the conquering of fear by faith."[8]

So take courage. Step out into the worlds of others. Stepping out will cause our world vision and our view of our great God to increase!

NOTES:
1. Franklin Graham, *Bob Pierce: This One Thing I Do* (Waco, Texas: Word, Inc., 1983), page 81.

2. For information on the resettlement of refugees, write to World Relief Commission, P.O. Box WRC, Wheaton, Illinois 60189.
3. This is one of the mottos of International Students Incorporated, a ministry that specializes in reaching international students with the love of Christ. Information on this ministry can be obtained by writing to them at P.O. Box C, Colorado Springs, Colorado 80901.
4. Lawson Lau, *The World at Your Doorstep* (Downers Grove, Illinois: InterVarsity Press, 1984), pages 12-13.
5. Don Bjork, "Foreign Missions: Next Door and Down the Street," *Christianity Today* (July 12, 1985), page 17.
6. As quoted by Philip Yancey in "Gandhi and Christianity," *Christianity Today* (April 8, 1983), page 16.
7. John Pollock, *Hudson Taylor and Maria* (Grand Rapids: Zondervan Publishing House, 1962), page 127.
8. James Buchan, *The Expendable Mary Slessor* (New York: Seabury Press, 1981), page 136.

Fellowship

"But encourage [or exhort] one another daily, as long as it is called Today, so that none of you may be hardened by sin's deceitfulness" (Hebrews 3:13). Most of us enjoy being encouraged, but few of us enjoy exhortation. Exhortation communicates the idea of being corrected or reprimanded. Yet in the biblical sense, such correction or exhortation is necessary to stimulate growth.

Our world vision is further built when we, in Christian fellowship groups, encourage each other to think beyond ourselves. The reason for exhortation is clearly expressed in Hebrews 3:13—so we do not become hardened by the deceitfulness of sin. Good Christian fellowship helps keep us from becoming hardened. When we "consider how we may spur one another on toward love and good deeds" (Hebrews 10:24), our attitudes will be softened. We can learn, through the gentle rebuke of fellow Christians, that the world does not revolve around our problems. Through others we can learn that there are bigger needs than our own.

In Christian fellowship, we exhort one another "as iron sharpens iron" (Proverbs 27:17). The sparks may fly, there may be a healthy clashing of our wills, but the end result is greater sharpness in our walk with the Lord. So true Christian fellowship should be a great stimulus toward a greater world vision. As we seek to know the Lord together and keep our world's needs before us, we are kept from the deceitfulness of self-centered sin.

Missions and world vision should be a focus of our fellowship because this is perhaps the most basic reason why we come together. A.R. Hay expresses the relationship of fellowship and missions this way:

> We present the Church from the missionary point of view. The missionary point of view is the only true one. The Lord founded the Church as a missionary organization. Such was its original structure. It was not an ecclesiastical organization with missionary endeavor as a department of its work. Missionaries were its leaders. Its primary purpose was missionary and all its members engaged in the propagation of the Gospel.[1]

FELLOWSHIP GROUPS GOD HAS USED IN MISSIONS

The history of missions is full of illustrations of fellowship groups whose members were willing to think beyond themselves in an effort to fulfill their part in God's worldwide plan.

The book of Acts demonstrates fellowship at its best. In Acts we read of men and women who were growing, learning from God's Word, and concerned about obeying God's commands. Together, these Christians were united when they were under persecution (Acts 4:1-31), and were unified as they released their members to go out in ministry (Acts 13:1-3). Ted Engstrom comments on the missions orientation of the early Church:

> The Book of Acts sets forth the church's initial
> response to Christ's missionary mandate given to his

disciples. It is clear from Scripture that the early church was fully aware of its assignment. In those days the church was mission, and the early history of the church was marked by its sense of mission. This was her inescapable calling as evidenced by the content of the entire Book of Acts.[2]

Modern missions provides many illustrations of missions-committed fellowships whose members were world Christians, too. In the early 1700s, the Moravian Movement, under the leadership of Count Nicolas Von Zinzendorf, began to take the Great Commission to heart as a united fellowship: "The all-consuming objective was to spread the Gospel to the ends of the earth, a passion that was clearly evident in their proportion of missionaries to lay people. The ratio was 1:60, a noteworthy attainment in comparison to the ratio of 1:5000 in Protestantism as a whole."[3] The Moravians stirred each other up, constantly keeping before them the idea that every Christian should act as a missionary. They had a world vision and a worldwide impact as a result.

In 1806, an event that has become known as the "Haystack Prayer Meeting" demonstrated God's ability to work through a group of individuals who were committed to making missions the focus of their fellowship. Ruth Tucker describes the event.

This outdoor prayer meeting, an unplanned event, was a landmark in American foreign missions. A group of missionary-minded Williams College students, known as the Society of the Brethren, were in the habit of meeting outside for prayer. Caught in a thunderstorm one afternoon, they took shelter under a nearby haystack. It was there under that haystack that they pledged themselves to missionary service.[4]

The first missionary sent out from North America, Adoniram Judson, came out of that prayer group.

In 1886, Dwight L. Moody and 251 students met at the Mount Hermon Conference. After a month of studying Scripture and exhorting one another concerning God's love for the world, 100 of the group committed themselves to world missions service. The Student Volunteer Movement, which was born at that meeting, sent out thousands of missionaries over the next thirty years. They went out under the slogan, "The evangelization of the world in this generation!"

From the Cambridge Seven (from which C.T. Studd emerged) to the Moravians, from the Christians of Acts to the Wheaton College Class of 1949 (which produced Jim Elliot, David Howard, and others), the testimony is clear; building a world vision is a cooperative effort. A world-oriented fellowship group can build up individual members and give the group a healthy, outward focus. The testimony of The Navigators and Campus Crusade echo the words of InterVarsity Christian Fellowship, "Christian student work will die without missions."[5] We can, and should, stir each other up to greater involvement in the world around us.

BUILDING WORLD VISION IN FELLOWSHIP GROUPS

Theologian Emil Brunner is credited with saying, "The church exists by mission as a fire exists by burning." Another way to say this is: Without missions, our church or fellowship is missing the reason for its existence.

We need to build a zeal and interest in missions in our churches and fellowship groups. But we need to know how to grow in practical ways. We need to learn how to develop a cooperative, corporate world vision. The following six suggestions can help create a more missions-oriented, world vision-building fellowship:

1. Incorporate the building blocks described in this book into the fellowship. A Bible study on God's worldwide plan, a cooperative study on a current issue, or a group trip to an international restaurant can do wonders for a fellowship group that is too inwardly centered.

2. Pray about missions together. J. Robertson McQuilkin believes that one of the greatest reasons the Church of Jesus Christ has not completed the Great Commission is due to our lack of prayer together. He asks, "Are we not weak in our impact for God because we are weak in time spent with God?"[6] Fellowship group prayer is a positive step to correct this problem.

3. Adopt a giving project together. One source documents that the average Christian gives less than fifteen dollars per year to missions.[7] Why is this amount so low? I believe one basic reason is our failure to stir each other up to give to missions. We tolerate mediocrity in our fellowship group because we do not want to "step on anyone else's toes." In reality, we need to offer "open rebukes" (Proverbs 27:5-6) to each other so we can develop and grow in all areas, including our giving.

In one of the tightest fellowship situations I have ever experienced (a team that went together to Kenya), we stirred each other up to give. Rather than spending all our team money on ourselves, we gave a sizable gift to a Bible college student from Chad. With our gift, she was able to pay for her room, board, tuition, and books for one year! Our fellowship group grew because of what we did together.

4. Work together. Many of our fellowship groups suffer from nearsightedness, the tendency to see only our own needs. We come together to pray for our own concerns, study the Bible for our own enrichment, and share our own burdens with each other. None of this is wrong; it is simply too narrow an understanding of fellowship.

Fellowship should be a common sharing of life together, which could include working on a missions project together or researching a missionary's work. It could also mean going out together to share Christ's love with the people right around us.

Fellowship involves building our lives together so we can be sent out into the world. Henri Nouwen explains the importance of doing this together: "Mission work is not a task for individuals. The Lord sent his disciples into the world in small groups, not as individual heroes or pioneers. We are sent out together, so that together—gathered by One Lord—we can make him present in this world."[8]

5. *Adopt a project together.* A missionary, country, or people group can all be subjects of a fellowship group's outward focus. The healthy fellowship groups I know of focus on international student outreach or the church behind the Iron Curtain. These groups do not exist for themselves alone. They pray for, give to, and are involved in mission activities so that their world visions will expand.

6. *Send someone out.* Dr. Paul Beals says, "The local church must take the initiative as the sending authority for missionaries."[9] Yet many churches and fellowship groups fall far short of this challenge.

One reason for this shortfall is the lack of a sending mentality in our fellowship groups. If we are to build such a mentality, we must start with ourselves. This might mean sending our pastor to a cross-cultural location. Such an experience will not only encourage the missionaries he visits, but will serve to make missions a basic ingredient of church fellowship.

Sending a group member out will intensify our prayers for specific needs, increase our interest in the part of the world to which the member goes, and challenge our financial participation.

MORE SUGGESTIONS FOR EFFECTIVE VISION BUILDING

Most of us aspire to have fellowship groups and churches that have greater vision for and commitment to world evangelization. As we build such a vision together, we need to keep several principles in mind.

First, remember that our goal is to build a greater outward focus, not to ignore each other. Fellowship groups need to pray for world needs in addition to personal needs, not instead of these needs. Some groups overreact to the self-centeredness of their past by ignoring each other's needs as they begin to focus attention on missions. A better response is to seek balance between inward and outward focus.

When we build a greater outward focus, our fellowship groups begin to function like teams on a mission. We care for each other so we can be more effective in fulfilling our role in the world. "With a global life-or-death cause before it, a support group won't settle for being just a collection of individuals. It will be a team-on-a-mission that has integrated its caring and fellowship into the world-wide mission of Christ Himself. Fellowship will be more the by-product of such a team than its purpose."[10]

Second, make learning together fun. Quizzes, geographical games, and other missions-related learning (see building block ten) can enhance a group's overall commitment to missions.

Through our church's children's ministry, families grow in their commitment to missions and world vision because we make learning fun. Families come to an annual missionary project that summarizes what class members have been learning all year. The most recent project took our children "Around the World in Eighty Minutes." The project enabled children and their families to visit displays about missionaries from six continents. The pictures, artifacts, and interaction made the learning experience a lot of fun.

For our youth group, we planned a fellowship meeting with a missions focus. Although missions is usually viewed as boring to most teens, our youth group's vision for missions was intensified that night because we made it fun. Rather than starting the meeting with a missions speaker, we divided the teens into groups for a " 'Round the World" obstacle course. Using a few simple props, chairs, a room divider, and tape on the floor, relay teams had to "crawl across the Sahara," "jump over the international dateline," "scale the Himalayas," and "run across the Great Wall of China." After traveling " 'Round the World," the group was ready to learn about missions.

A third suggestion is to make our missions world-vision growth manageable. If we belong to a church or fellowship group that has had no missions zeal in the past, we cannot expect a change to occur overnight. In such instances we need to start small. Progress for one group might be to eat Mexican food or to buy a world map. Remember, more people are stimulated to develop their world visions by those who start small and build than by those who insist on a radical reversal of priorities.

A fourth suggestion is to realize that building a world vision is a commitment. We cannot be discouraged if everyone is not as interested in or motivated to build a world vision as we are.

Since the nature of missions is sacrifice (see Philippians 2:5ff), it is not easy to get people excited about missions. As one writer bluntly says, "The modern church fails [in missions] because 'missionary' has become a dirty word."[11] Missions is not a popular topic; it is much easier to be concerned about my needs, my hurts, and my interests than it is to care about God's world. So building a missions or world vision in our fellowship groups is a commitment. Remembering this helps us persevere when we are tempted to give up.

Fifth, we must see ourselves as "infecting" agents. A vision for world missions spreads like a virus or bacteria. If we are ourselves "infected," we will be able to "infect" others. As we become healthier with respect to seeing the world as God does, we will be able to bring health to others. We cannot blame a lack of missions enthusiasm on others. Instead, we should see ourselves as God's positive agents of change who can help our brothers and sisters grow with us. Together we can start seeing the world with God's compassion.

Finally, we will do our best to influence others if we let God direct our steps regarding missions. Maybe He wants to instill a missions vision in our fellowship group or church by sending us somewhere in the world. Are we open to this possibility? If not, then our commitment to a world vision begins to sound shallow and insincere.

The great Baptist preacher, Charles Haddon Spurgeon, challenged his students by saying,

> We ought to put it on this footing—not "Can I prove that I *ought* to go?" but "Can I prove that I *ought not* to go?" When a man can prove honestly that he ought not to go then he is clear, but not else. What answer do you give, my brethren?[12]

If we are interested in missions, we too should take this challenge to heart.

As the minister in charge of directing others in our church toward missions, I am frequently asked, "If you are so committed to the needs around the world, why are you still here?" For now I can answer this excellent question with a definitive sense of calling to stay. However, if I am to continue to challenge others effectively regarding a world vision, I must regularly be willing to consider this basic question about God's call in my life.

AN OUTWARDLY-FOCUSED FELLOWSHIP

The people in our fellowship are great resources in keeping me from becoming "hardened" by my own deceitful self-centeredness. By exhorting me, my friend Larry causes me to think about the hidden people of the world.[13] Tom stimulates me to think about international students in our area, and Mary Ann reminds me of the needs of the inner city. My fellowship partners stir me up to good works so that together we might achieve the full potential of our fellowship.

A.R. Hay describes the nature of the New Testament church as, "a center of light and power, its energy radiating not inwardly but outwards. Its power is the Holy Spirit's dynamic power, exercised in and through each member for the accomplishment of Christ's command that His message of salvation be taken to the ends of the earth and to every creature."[14]

If we keep our perspectives straight, we, too, shall radiate Christ's love outward so that our fellowship groups and churches can be the caring, sending groups that God intends them to be.

NOTES:
1. Alexander Rattrey Hay, *The New Testament Order for Church and Missionary* (Audubon, New Jersey: New Testament Missionary Union, n.d.), page 136.
2. Ted W. Engstrom, *What in the World Is God Doing?* (Waco, Texas: Word, Inc., 1978), page 203.
3. Ruth A. Tucker, *From Jerusalem to Irian Jaya* (Grand Rapids: Zondervan Publishing House, 1983), page 69.
4. Tucker, page 122.
5. David Bryant, *In the Gap* (Downers Grove, Illinois: InterVarsity Press, 1979), page 68.
6. J. Robertson McQuilkin, *The Great Omission* (Grand Rapids: Baker Book House, 1984), page 63.
7. Samuel Wilson and Gordon Aeschliman, *The Hidden Half* (Monrovia, California: MARC, n.d.), page 118.
8. Henri Nouwen, *¡Gracias! A Latin American Journal* (New York: Harper and Row, 1983), page 43.

9. Paul Beals, *A People For His Name* (Pasadena, California: William Carey Library, 1985), page 75.
10. Bryant, page 64.
11. J.D. Douglas, ed. *Let the Earth Hear His Voice* (Minneapolis: World Wide Publications, 1975), page 166.
12. Charles H. Spurgeon, *Lectures to My Students* (Grand Rapids: Zondervan Publishing House, 1970), page 217.
13. The term "hidden peoples" is attributed to Dr. Ralph Winter in reference to more than 16,000 people groups who have not received the proclamation of the gospel.
14. Hay, page 296.

Giving

As Americans, we are the financially rich people of the world. We have more resources, more discretionary money, and more possessions than most of the world's people. We may not always feel rich, at least in comparison to our neighbors, but we are—especially if we compare ourselves to the rest of the world's population.

Ronald Sider has prophetically drawn our attention to this fact by highlighting the plight of the world's hungry. He writes,

> Ten thousand persons died today because of inadequate food. One billion people are mentally retarded or physically deformed because of a poor diet. The problem, we know, is that the world's resources are not evenly distributed. North Americans live on an affluent island amid a sea of starving humanity.[1]

Sounds pessimistic, doesn't it? Yes, but we can become part of the actual solution if we begin to consider it a great privilege to be financially involved with our world. While not a substitute for personal involvement, financial participation is one way we who are rich can invest in the Church's worldwide ministry outreach.

Jesus tells us that our hearts and treasure are directly linked: "For where your treasure is, there your heart will be also" (Matthew 6:21). Thus, if we want to develop a heart for world missions, we should direct our earthly treasure that way as well. Giving to missions and worldwide concerns also enhances our prayer for missions. Although it sounds harsh to admit it, we tend to pray more for the ministries that are connected to our checkbooks. We pray for what we pay for!

THE BIBLICAL MANDATE REGARDING MONEY

One of the greatest joys of understanding God's Word is finding out that it is eminently practical. The commands of Scripture apply to our daily lives on the most basic levels. This practicality is very evident when it comes to the issue of money and how we handle our resources. God makes His will clear in a variety of respects.

1. God wants us to be generous. In Malachi 3:8-10, the people of Israel were rebuked for refusing to present the tithe (ten percent) to the Lord as an offering. In so doing, they violated a basic admonition of the Law and even the pre-Law example of Abraham, who tithed to Melchizedek (Genesis 14:18-20; Leviticus 27:30; Numbers 18:21,24; Deuteronomy 26:12). The people were taught to bring their tithes as a physical reminder that everything they had belonged to God.

In the New Testament, however, the teaching on the tithe is not repeated, a fact that has caused many Christians to consider the tithe to be nonapplicable to Christians who are "not under the Law but under grace."

Indeed, Christians are not legally bound to the Law's requirements, but, as Dr. Harold Lindsell points out in the *Harper Study Bible,* "The Christian can do no less for God under grace than the Jew did under Law. The tithe is therefore an outward evidence of an inward commitment and springs from one's love for God."[2]

The hesitant giver might respond, "Okay, but do I tithe before taxes or after taxes?" This question indicates that the person has missed a basic teaching of Scripture. God is not concerned about the letter of the Law; He wants us to be generous. The biblical philosophy on giving is clearly stated in 2 Corinthians 9:6-7:

> Remember this: Whoever sows sparingly will also reap sparingly, and whoever sows generously will also reap generously. Each man should give what he has decided in his heart to give, not reluctantly or under compulsion, *for God loves a cheerful giver.* (emphasis added)

Dr. Oswald J. Smith, whose leadership of the People's Church of Toronto led his church members to give millions of dollars to missions, lived according to Peter Marshall's words: "Give according to your income lest God make your income according to your giving."[3]

The principle of generosity stems from the same root as the Old Testament teaching on the tithe: *all* we have belongs to God. By giving we express our understanding of that fact and show our submission to our Lord.

2. God measures our responsible stewardship by our response to the poor and needy. "The crucial test" of stewardship, says Ronald Sider, "is whether the prosperous are obeying God's command to bring justice to the oppressed."[4] Such an observation comes from paying full attention to the Scriptures, especially those that tend to make us feel uncomfortable. Consider these examples from Scripture:

Genesis 1:26-31: God gives man all good things for the purpose of benefiting the whole world (stewardship).

Psalm 112:1-9: the faithful worshiper of God is richly blessed, and "his righteousness endures forever" because "he has scattered abroad his gifts to the poor."

Proverbs 31:10ff: the wise woman does very well in business (verses 14,16,18), and she is marked by the fact that she "opens her arms to the poor" (verse 20).

Amos 2:6-8: the wealthy are condemned because they "trample on the heads of the poor . . . and deny justice to the oppressed."

Matthew 25:31-46: God's judgment is seen in direct correlation to an individual's response to the poor, needy, homeless, etc., because that poor person represents Christ Himself.

Luke 16:19-31: the rich man is rebuked after his death because of his ill treatment of the poor man, Lazarus.

1 Timothy 6:17-19: those who are rich in this life are instructed to be "rich in good deeds, and to be generous and willing to share" so that they can lay up a treasure for themselves for the coming age.

Scripture is clear; whatever wealth we have received is to be used to benefit others. Such generosity is the only correct use of wealth.

3. God wants us to keep the Kingdom of God as our top priority. Jesus' teaching about the connection between our hearts and possessions (Matthew 6:21) is followed by His basic instruction to "seek first his kingdom" (Matthew 6:33).

The writer, Agur, in Proverbs 30, prays that God will keep him from the extremes of poverty or riches. Poverty may incite him to steal, but riches may make him feel self-sufficient and cause him to deny his need for the Lord (verses 7-9). Through Agur, God teaches us that riches are deceitful and can cause us to lose our spiritual focus. Obedience requires that we maintain a sense of dependence on the Lord.

A third example of our need to make God's Kingdom our top priority is Jesus' encounter with the rich, young ruler (see Matthew 19:16-26, Mark 10:17-27, Luke 18:18-27). The young man is turned away not because of his riches *per se,* but because his priorities are not in correct alignment with the Lord's. His riches hold his heart.

The challenge to "seek first his kingdom" is a daily one that we all face. We show our desire to keep this priority in order by the way we use our possessions and resources.

FINANCIAL GIVING WITH A WORLD VISION

Giving to increase our world vision should occur in at least two forms: money and time. The most basic giving is, of course, out of our financial resources. When we give of our financial resources, however, we cannot respond to every need nor can we take the matter lightly. We must seek to be faithful stewards of all that God has given us. This should mean careful research into where we send our money and follow-up on how it is used.

The seven principles of giving outlined below will help increase effective management of our financial resources.

1. We need a personal financial strategy. Each person needs to decide what his or her measure of generosity will be. After deciding this, the person must choose how the money will be distributed. Ministries and Christian workers close to home—including our commitment to our own local church— must be taken into consideration as well as financial opportunities overseas.

The basic rule of thumb, however, is this—we need a predetermined plan. If we let appeal letters or crises determine how we use our money, we will give in an erratic, undisciplined fashion. We need to know how we are going to use our money so we can have a distinct sense of being responsible with the money the Lord has given us.

2. We need to have some targets for giving. If our strategy helps us determine how we want to use our money, our targets help us decide where we will use it, especially overseas. We should not give one dollar per year to a thousand different ministries just to feel that we are involved in many ministries. We need specific targets, places where we believe God wants us to be involved.

Some people may decide to target their gifts to ministries or missionaries in a particular geographic location. Others may choose a specific type of work to support—like student work, church planting, or Bible translation. Still others may choose a well-distributed balance, giving significantly to a few diverse ministries in various locations.

My wife and I have decided to distribute our money given for overseas work according to a rough ratio of seventy percent people versus thirty percent project. We regularly support a few missionaries throughout the year, and then—once a year or a few times during the year—we give other accumulated money to a designated project (or projects) in which we believe we should participate.

3. We need to check on the financial responsibility of the agencies (or people) to which we give. To be responsible stewards is work, and this includes the work we need to do after our money is given. We should check to see that the dollars we send are being used in the way we had intended, and we should look for responsible accounting and reporting practices.

One of the most difficult experiences I have ever had with respect to missions occurred because of financial mismanagement on behalf of the mission agency. At the outset of our involvement, I was a little suspicious when the agency could not provide an accurate accounting of receipts or financial records, but my opinions were confirmed when I found out that the United States Post Office was charging the president of the mission with a variety of counts of mail fraud. Fortunately, we found out about the situation before our gifts were misused.

One way to make sure that money is being used responsibly is to look for the logo "ECFA" on the mission letterhead. These letters signify that the mission belongs to the "Evangelical Council for Financial Accountability," an agency dedicated to helping Christian ministries be faithful in their use and reporting of funds.

If our money is given to individuals (or to ministries that do not belong to ECFA), the best way to make sure that the money is being used in the desired way is to ask. Many times we are afraid that asking about the money we give makes it seem that we have not really given it, but holding others accountable for their use of funds is part of our stewardship.

4. We need to periodically evaluate where our money is going. On one occasion, I discovered that I was giving to a project that had been completed six months earlier. (Why the missionary had not told me this, I still do not know.) The money I sent was simply being put into the mission's general fund. While I had no objection to helping the mission generally, my intent was to be more specific in my giving. Through that experience, I learned to check more carefully to make sure that past commitments are still connected to ongoing needs.

Periodically evaluating where our money is going is also a good way to keep current on the targets and strategies we have chosen for the funds we give. If we are willing to evaluate, we may choose new targets or we may choose to alter our strategy. If we do not evaluate, we can fall prey to the temptation to give without really caring about the ministries or people we support.

5. We need to become involved with the ministries we

support. Such involvement could mean personal activity, like a visit to the mission field. It might mean reminding the mission leaders to have vision, remembering Hudson Taylor's words, "God's work done in God's way will never lack supplies."[5]

For many missionaries at our church, the quarterly check can be quite impersonal. They know that we support them, but they would rather know who is sending the money. Thus, our letters and phone calls can help them connect the gifts to the givers, and the missionaries feel more cared for.

6. *We need to sacrifice.* We must not take the encouragement to have a strategy and target our giving as a reason to reduce our giving to a mechanical science. There must be room for the Holy Spirit to lead us to give beyond what we plan to give. There must be an openness to sacrifice.

On the most basic level, sacrifice could mean being willing to live at a lower standard of living than we are capable of so we can give more away. It could mean giving away that "something extra" (like an end-of-year bonus, an expected windfall, or an unusually high tax return) rather than thinking of ways to spend the amount on ourselves.

On a deeper level, sacrifice means realizing that all we have is the Lord's, and we should be willing to let Him direct our giving. We sing the hymn, "Take my life . . ." and we boldly say, "Take my silver and my gold: not a mite would I withhold."[6] When God calls us to sacrifice, we find out if we really mean those words.

7. *Pray.* Giving reminds us that God is in control, that He owns everything (including us), and that we are simply stewards. Therefore, the final basic aspect of responsible giving is prayer—another way we demonstrate our submission to the Lord.

When we pray about our giving, we should not simply say, "Lord, this is what I am going to give and where I am going to give it." Instead, we should open ourselves up to hear His voice and direction. We should come to the Lord with an open mind and an open checkbook, asking, "Lord, how much? Lord, where? Lord, to whom?" When we place our giving plans at the Lord's feet, we can be sure that He will direct our steps.

GIVING OUR TIME WITH A WORLD VISION

Giving must also include our other great resource, time. Giving of time includes time given in service to our local church, time used to prepare to teach others, and time spent in witnessing (and the accompanying relationship-building) to our nonChristian friends.

The giving of time is also instrumental in building a world vision. Some people give two weeks per year of vacation time to assist missionary friends overseas. Others volunteer to type, file, or do administrative work at the home offices of mission agencies. Still others choose to use their retirement years for missionary service rather than opting for the comfortable vision of retirement at a beachfront resort.

If we choose to build a vision for God's world, we will have to make a sacrifice of time. Prayer, research, reading, and careful stewardship all take time. Getting firsthand experience also takes time and money.

The Jacobis, for example, chose to use some of their time to visit missionaries. As a result, they sacrificed some family vacation time, but have been greatly enriched as they have grown close to a missionary family. The Lindstroms sacrificed some of their vacation time to visit a mission school. On a business trip, Mr. Stephenson took time out of a busy schedule to call a missionary at an out-of-the-way mission station.

In all three of these cases, the people involved sacrificed and made a time investment. The result has been increased prayer for certain missionaries and a greater vision for the world. The sacrifice is worth it!

WHAT HAPPENS WHEN WE GIVE?

Whether it involves our time or money, giving—especially generous giving—provides some excellent benefits as we grow with respect to world vision.

First, when we give money to ministries in the developing world, we realize just how far our money can go. On one occasion, our church missions budget gave $3,000 toward a pastors' conference in Colombia, South America. After the conference, our missionary contact wrote to tell us how our money was used (a good example of accountability).

He told us that our gift of $3,000 had totally paid for a three-day, two-night conference at the Caribbean Bible Center for more than 200 pastors—including their food! As if this was not already testimony enough to the way our dollars were stretched, he went on to say, "With the money left over, there will be a follow-up conference for some of the leaders in February."

We have the privilege of literally *investing* our money in ministries overseas and seeing how far God can use it. When we see how far our money can go, we are encouraged to be even more generous.

Second, when we are involved in worldwide giving, we become increasingly aware of the fact that God has blessed us and the United States with an unusual stockpile of resources and money. We see that it is our job to be responsible in our use of these resources.

I became acutely aware of our available resources when I visited the Moffat College of Bible in Kenya, which is a training school for East African pastors. This school had sixty students in cramped quarters, each of whom would go on to become a pastor and lead five to eight churches. When I asked why there were not more students, the answer was clear: no money meant no facilities, and no facilities meant no increase in the size of the student body.

The only thing they lacked was financial resources. They had willing students waiting to be admitted. They had (in this case) a faculty who could teach them. They had dozens of churches that were hungry for pastors to help them, but they lacked money. When I found out that they could almost double their facilities for about $50,000 (one-half of the amount we spent on our church organ, and a fraction of the cost of any of our buildings), I was reminded of Jesus' words that "from everyone who has been given much, much will be demanded" (Luke 12:48).

The question we who are wealthy will consistently face as we get serious about world missions giving is this: How can we be most responsible for all that we have been given?

Third, when we commit ourselves to giving in a way that builds our vision for the world, we will become acutely aware of the need to make world evangelization a priority for ourselves, our churches, and our fellowships.

Oswald J. Smith challenges us to give to missions through these four observations:

1. If I refuse to give anything to missions this year, I practically cast a ballot in favor of the recall of every missionary.

2. If I give less than heretofore, I favor the reduction of the missionary forces proportionate to my reduced contribution.

3. If I give the same as formerly, I favor holding the ground already won; but I oppose any forward movement. My song is "Hold the Fort," forgetting that the Lord never intended His army to take refuge in a

fort. All His soldiers are commanded to "Go!"

4. If I increase my offering beyond former years, then I favor an advance movement in the conquest of new territory for Christ.[7]

God richly blesses us by giving us the choice to increase our missions involvement through giving our resources. May God give us the grace to respond with generosity, even as He has been generous with us.

NOTES:
1. Ronald Sider, *Rich Christians in an Age of Hunger* (Downers Grove, Illinois: InterVarsity Press, 1977), page 172.
2. Harold Lindsell, ed., *Harper Study Bible* (Grand Rapids: Zondervan Publishing House, 1964), page 1426.
3. Oswald J. Smith, *The Challenge of Missions* (Bromley, England: STL Books, 1959), page 59.
4. Sider, page 128.
5. John Pollock, *Hudson Taylor and Maria* (Grand Rapids: Zondervan Publishing House, 1964), page 75.
6. "Take My Life, and Let It Be," *Hymns II* (Downers Grove, Illinois: InterVarsity Press, 1976), page 112.
7. Smith, page 69.

Meeting Missionaries

When Paul and Barnabas returned from their first missionary journey, "they gathered the church together and reported all that God had done through them and how he had opened the door of faith to the Gentiles" (Acts 14:27). Perhaps this report stirred the missionary interest of John Mark; it definitely stimulated the early Church in its world vision and provided the foundation for others to be sent out.

If we want to build our world visions, we must be in touch with those who are involved in cross-cultural, world-wide ministries. Our personal contact with missionaries can come through newsletters or visits with them when they are on furlough. We need this interaction so we can pray more intelligently and so God can challenge us to consider missions involvement. We also need interaction with missionaries so we can break down our false ideas about what missionary work is really like. Many of us have dated, unrealistic pictures about missions work, and our images need to be rectified.

In his book, *Fred 'n' Erma,* Calvin Miller presents a humorous look at what might be our own false ideas about missionaries through a conversation between Fred and Dawn Marie:

DAWN MARIE: Daddy, what do missionaries do all day?

FRED: Well, they get up early, sweetheart, and tiptoe through the jungle shooting monkeys till they find a native, and then they tell him to get some clothes on if he wants to become a Christian.

DAWN MARIE: And do they do it?

FRED: Sometimes they do and sometimes they don't.

DAWN MARIE: My Sunday school teacher said that she prays for a missionary in Lagos and that they have buses and airports just like we do.

FRED: Oh, I don't think so, honey! They don't even have frozen dinners or baseball cards!

DAWN MARIE: Oh, then they must be very poor.

FRED: Yes, you can't have hardly any money or they won't let you live in Africa. If they had much money, they would want Adidas and Corvettes, and it's hard to want to be a Christian once you get a Corvette. Missionaries are poor too. They only get one camera and enough money to buy film so they can take pictures of monkeys and sunsets.

DAWN MARIE: Daddy, are there lots of snakes in the jungles?

FRED: Of course, and no missionary can even be ordained until he wrestles a twenty-five-foot anaconda and pins him three times. If you can get one skinned it's all the better because you have something to hang over the piano in American churches on missionary night. One time the Whiteheads of Swaziland had leather coats they had made from wildebeests and iguana belts made from iguanas they had found in their beds right after they said their prayers. That's why missionaries pray so much; it helps keep the iguanas over in the natives' beds.[1]

PERSONAL ENCOUNTERS BREAK DOWN STEREOTYPES

We all have false ideas about what missionaries do. Although we may not be as narrow-minded or as misguided as Fred, we may need to correct notions of missionaries "shooting monkeys in Madagascar."[2]

Some of us believe that all missionaries are "super-spiritual" types who come close to walking on water, a belief that can actually hinder our growth as world Christians. This false image may be perpetuated by the way we put missionaries on a pedestal, but it is a destructive stereotype that makes us think missions work is far beyond our spiritual capacities. This false idea also hurts our relationships with missionaries because we assume that they do not hurt, sin, or fail like we do.

Others (although few would admit it) believe that missionaries are people who "couldn't really make it in our culture, so they went someplace else." Franklin Graham, the son of evangelist Billy Graham, probably met dozens of missionaries when he was young, yet he admits to having a very negative picture of them:

> The Annoor Hospital in Mafraq, Jordan, is where I got my vision for missions. When I was eighteen, I heard about this particular hospital and the need they had for an automobile. The Palestine Liberation Organization (PLO) had stolen the missionaries' car. Until then, my understanding of missions was only what I observed when missionaries came home on furlough: if narrow lapels were in style, they had wide lapels; if narrow ties were in style, they had wide ties; if they told jokes, they were always jokes that had been told four years earlier. That was my impression of missionaries—people who were always out of style.[3]

Either extreme view of missionaries—the "super-spiritual" image or the out-of-style "loser" image—is harmful to the growth of our world vision. It is very difficult to be excited about world missions if we are repulsed or overwhelmed by our impression of missionaries.

The best way to correct these false ideas is through firsthand involvement with missionaries. The thought that missionaries are "super-spiritual" or "out-of-date" is the result of too many superficial contacts. We fail to let these cross-cultural workers increase our vision because we fail to get to know them personally.

His trip to the Annoor Hospital in Jordan helped Franklin Graham change his ideas about missionaries. After he worked with the missionaries in Jordan, he said, "I discovered that these missionaries were not out of style at all, but were serving God at great personal sacrifice. I had been judging all missionaries by their outward appearance, but God looks at one's heart."[4]

MISSIONARIES CAN TELL US ABOUT GOD'S WORK

If we want to grow through our personal relationships with missionaries, we must be willing to go beyond superficial encounters and erroneous assumptions so we can know and learn from these special teachers.

"Reporting back" is a biblical concept. We see it in the example of Saul and Barnabas (cf. Acts 14, referred to earlier), the example of the disciples Jesus sent out (Luke 10:1-20), and the example of the spies that Moses sent into the Promised Land (Deuteronomy 1:19-25). These biblical examples instruct us regarding what we should look for in our personal meetings with missionaries. Two themes seem evident in the biblical examples.

First, it is evident that they gave their reports to those

who sent them in order to encourage the faith of others by detailing what God had done. In Acts, Saul and Barnabas reported "all that God had done through them" (14:27). The disciples Jesus sent out reported with excitement that, "Lord, even the demons submit to us in your name" (Luke 10:17). The focus of this reporting was to build faith by revealing God's work.

The second reason for reporting back is to give the senders vision. This may be part of the missionary team's report in Acts 14. It is certainly the reason behind the spies' reports after they looked over the Promised Land: "It is a good land that the LORD our God is giving us" (Deuteronomy 1:25).

As exemplified in these biblical accounts, we need to expand our world vision and understanding of missions by hearing directly from those who work in other lands and cultures. Their firsthand reports help build our faith as we hear what God is doing, and they help us have vision so we can intensify our prayers or consider where God might want to send us.

If we are going to understand what God is doing in our world, and are going to understand the people through whom He acts, we must get to know some of the missionaries who are out on the front lines.

HOW TO GET TO KNOW A MISSIONARY

Breaking down our false notions of who missionaries are and what they do is the first step in meeting them for the purpose of expanding our vision. There are six good ways to do this as we march toward our world vision goal.

1. Start receiving a missionary newsletter. Most missionaries publish a newsletter three or four times a year. These are excellent tools to help us understand God's work through a missionary (or missionary family). Newsletters can also help us understand the particular challenges missionaries face. A recent newsletter from missionary friends in Mozambique contained both elements.

Stuart and Sindia Foster, missionaries located in the capital city of Maputo, wrote about God's work in Mozambique. In one location, where they were starting to build a church building, the people showed up to help. When Stuart came by one afternoon, sixty people gathered at the construction site and asked him to preach. A spontaneous service ensued, indicative of the people's spiritual hunger.

The spiritual awakening, however, is accompanied by great hardships for the Fosters. Sindia writes,

> Our daily lives would seem curious to you. Cara [their infant daughter] has her bath by candlelight and sleeps under mosquito netting, often still getting bitten by fleas or mosquitos. I wash diapers and clothes every day by hand, hang them out at noon, and plan to be home a few hours to guard them. Food spoils so quickly, as the days get hotter and hotter—it's frustrating to throw out food in such a poor country and yet it is hard to find ways to store it. We have very few fresh fruits and vegetables, and we need to import most of our food (which means expensive delays and lots of canned food). Stuart's "schedule" is totally unpredictable and time off quite rare.

In the midst of a great movement of God's Spirit, we see accompanying hardship. Staying in touch with missionary newsletters can help us understand both aspects of a missionary's work.

2. Write personal letters. I have very seldom heard complaints from missionaries that they get "too much personal mail." As a matter of fact, most would long for more personal mail because for many, personal letters are the best way to find out about the churches and communities they have left behind.

"But what do I write?" This is the most common question people ask when I encourage them to get in touch with a missionary by mail. It might not sound too exotic, but my recommendation is to write about personal matters. Telling missionaries how God is at work in our lives, explaining the challenges our church is facing, or relating what we are studying can be very encouraging and uplifting. We should also be willing to talk about the "average" parts of our lives—weather, marriages in the church, and people coming and going. These ordinary events can all be part of good correspondence with missionaries.

When we write we must also demonstrate our concern for the missionary. A specific reference to a newsletter prayer request is a great encouragement to a missionary. It lets the missionary know that someone has read the letter and prayed over it. Asking the missionary about victories and defeats that he or she is facing is another way to show our concern.

Russ and Alberta Reinert, veteran missionaries in Peru with Wycliffe Bible Translators, were home recently. They told me how one of our laymen, Jack Strong, ministers to them. "Over the past ten years," they told me, "Jack has written to us every month with news of the church and his own family. He has kept us informed, and he has made us feel like we were really a part of the church family."

Personal correspondence built Jack's vision for Peru and the Reinerts' work. It also served to encourage the Reinerts in their ministry in another culture.

3. How about a phone call? I was amazed the other day to pick up my telephone, dial a long list of numbers, and hear the voice of a missionary in South America. Modern technology can bring immediate firsthand missions experience right into our homes!

Effective phone calling requires advance planning, however. I do not recommend a casual attitude that says, "Let's see how the Jones are doing today," and then calling someplace at a rate of five dollars per minute. Overseas phone calling takes planning, especially if we call locations where no one but our missionary friends can speak English. It is costly to call only to learn that they are not in the office.

Just the thought of being able to call almost anywhere in the world builds my world vision, but there should be more purpose to a call than just adventure. A phone call in response to an emergency is certainly a good idea. Or how about calling on a missionary's birthday? A phone call just to offer encouragement may be in order, but remember to plan ahead.

Our friend, Lesley, was teaching English in northern China. We could tell from her letters that she was becoming discouraged by the hard work, weather, and a variety of other factors. We wrote to her and asked if we could call and made arrangements for her to call us collect from a hotel in Harbin. Making allowances for the time difference, the plan was set.

On Saturday morning, the phone rang. It was the overseas operator asking if we would accept the collect call. We did, and we were connected with Lesley. She sounded a million miles away (she was only 12,000!); the connection was poor, and we spent a good portion of the hour yelling, "Are you still there?" Nevertheless, Lesley was encouraged, and we were stimulated by learning in the most direct way possible how we could pray for her and her teaching ministry. (Incidentally, the phone call cost us $105, so such encouragement is a once-per-year option for us!)

4. *Be faithful in prayer.* The most important thing a missionary can hear from us is, "I have been praying for you *every day.*" Our prayers are the evidence that we are truly

partners in ministry with them.

Prayer is also one of the best ways to get to know missionaries because God can teach us through prayer how we should pray for our friends in other cultures. Prayer is a time for intercession and a time for letting God lead our thoughts on how we should pray (see building block three).

5. *Invite missionaries into our home.* Letting our missionary friends live with us when they are home on furlough is one of the most effective ways we can get to know them and let them teach us about missions.

In the more formal atmosphere of church meetings, missionaries are often "official" in their presentations. In our homes, however, they can tell stories of victory and defeat; they can share the adventures that God is giving them in their lives and ministries; they can open our eyes to see God's hand at work in specific ways.

Hosting missionary friends also helps us gain a more intimate look at the realities our missionary friends face. In the relaxed atmosphere of our homes, they can share openly about the day-to-day challenges in their lives.

6. *Visit missionaries at their field of work.* My wife and I once made the long trek from Boston to Luampa, Zambia, to visit our church's missionaries, Bob and Joan Brain. We were exhausted by the traveling—two all-night flights; another two-hour flight from Nairobi, Kenya, to Lusaka, Zambia; and a seven-hour truck ride to the compound. At midnight we arrived at our missionaries' home; the lights were off (the generator shuts off at 10:00 p.m.), and they greeted us by candlelight.

In spite of our exhaustion, I distinctly remember Joan's first words: "We are so glad that you are here. You are the first people from any home church to visit us on the field in our twenty-five years in missions work."

Can you imagine serving for twenty-five years without

having one visitor from a supporting church? Indeed, it was not exactly an easy place to get to, but twenty-five years?

In light of the tremendous encouragement that a visit offers our missionaries, as well as the outstanding benefits for our own growth (see building block five), personal visits are something each of us should consider in our relationships with missionaries. A personal visit may not be as difficult as traveling to Luampa, Zambia; our visit may be to an inner-city worker who labors only twenty miles from our home. The point of such visits is two-fold.

First, a visit is our way of increasing our partnership with that missionary by coming into his or her world. In an effort to identify and understand the challenges of the missionary's particular ministry, we meet on his or her "home turf."

Second, a visit is our way of saying, "We know you are here." Many cross-cultural workers suffer from loneliness and the Elijah complex that, "I, only I, am left." A personal visit says we know and care about the work of that ministry.

DEEPENING OUR RELATIONSHIPS WITH MISSIONARIES

Building our missions vision through exposure to missionaries is a wonderful way to start a network of relationships all over the world. The challenge, however, is to keep these relationships fresh and growing.

Jim Elliot wrote, "Missionaries are very human folks, just doing what they are asked. Simply a bunch of nobodies trying to exalt Somebody."[5] Jim was making the point that missionaries are normal people; they are just like you and me! With this in mind we can build better and more effective relationships together. Consider these ideas for promoting growth between us and our missionary friends.

1. Ask them questions related to daily living. Their lives and culture might be very different from ours in some respects, but we will only find this out if we ask.

One of the most prevalent stereotypes in missions is that missionaries live in backward countries and spend a fair amount of time fighting off wild animals, tarantulas, or scorpions. If we ask questions about daily living, we may discover that our missionary friends live in modern cities, or that they have never seen a wild animal or tarantula during their tenure as missionaries.

2. *Do not generalize about missions or missionaries.* Some missionaries are quite overworked and others are—well—lazy.[6] (Remember, they are people just like us!) Some mission fields are full of revival and spiritual awakening; others are the "hard soil" where there seem to be few, if any, spiritual results.

3. *Ask about financial needs.* One of the saddest aspects of missions work is the way some missionaries are reduced to the point of begging for enough money to continue their ministries. We can put our missionary friends at ease by asking about their financial needs directly so they do not feel compelled to drop hints and hope that we get the message. We should ask directly and see if we can respond to their needs.

4. *Ask for specific prayer requests about their personal lives and families.* Henri Nouwen perceptively observes, "It is far from easy to be a missioner. One has to live in a different culture, speak a different language, and get used to a different climate, all at great distances from those patterns of life which fit most comfortably. It is not surprising that, for many missioners, life is full of tension, frustration, confusion, anxiety, alienation, and loneliness."[7]

We need to do our part—like the ground crew that keeps a plane in the air—in the ministry of missionaries by upholding them with specific prayers for their needs.

5. *Do not forget to ask about the missionary's spiritual*

life. Many of us erroneously assume that, since the missionary is doing the Lord's work, spiritual growth is automatic. Most missionaries will testify that this is far from true. In all types of missions work, Christian growth is still a struggle and a discipline.

Jim Harding, a veteran of more than fifteen years of missions work, met with me personally during one furlough. I asked him if there was anything we could do to improve our caring for him and his family.

"Yes," he replied emphatically, "please ask us next time, at the start of our visit, how we are doing spiritually." He explained that they had come home spiritually drained and had desperately wanted someone to care for them, but—because of our false assumption that all missionaries must be spiritual—we had failed to notice or ask about their spiritual need.

6. *Let God speak.* Encounters with missionaries are not simply for our personal growth in world vision. God may use these relationships as a way to call us out to cross-cultural service. Just as the report of the spies was intended to give vision to the people of Israel, the reports of our missionary friends may be God's way of communicating His vision to us.

CONCLUSION

One of the greatest aspects of my job is that I am required to meet personally with the missionaries our church supports whenever they are in our area. What a joy! I have had the thrill of meeting with people from all six continents. New missionaries and veterans alike help balance my vision regarding the challenges of missions today. Some missionaries work with isolated tribes; others work in great cities. A few work in the midst of spiritual revival; others persevere in the Muslim world where there are few observable results.

After every encounter with missionaries, I am encouraged to pray because I have faces to associate with the prayer letters. I can pray for specifics rather than offering a generic "bless the missionaries" prayer. I am challenged by the needs of our world. I also ask, "What about me? Is God directing me overseas or into another culture?" So far He has not, but my meetings with missionaries keep my heart open.

NOTES:

1. Calvin Miller, *Fred 'n' Erma* (Downers Grove, Illinois: InterVarsity Press, 1986), page 69.
2. "Shooting Monkeys in Madagascar" is the title of the second act of Miller's play, *Fred 'n' Erma.*
3. Franklin Graham, *Bob Pierce: This One Thing I Do* (Waco, Texas: Word, Inc., 1983), page 162.
4. Graham, page 163.
5. Elisabeth Elliot, *Shadow of the Almighty* (Grand Rapids: Zondervan Publishing House, 1958), page 46.
6. In her novel, *No Graven Image* (New York: Harper and Row, 1966), page 107, Elisabeth Elliot observes through the fictitious missionary, Margaret Sparhawk, "I once heard someone observe that a missionary could be the laziest or the most overworked person in the world. Here I saw both kinds."
7. Henri Nouwen, *¡Gracias! A Latin American Journal* (New York: Harper and Row, 1983), page 161.

Lifestyle Choices

How we choose to live and set our personal priorities conditions our ability to build our personal world vision. As stated in building block seven, our use of resources is directly aligned with our hearts' priorities. Where our treasure is, our heart will be (Matthew 6:21). A young woman once shared a dream with me: "The man I marry has to be rich," she said. With that kind of attitude—with wealth as her priority—she will have a difficult time taking her eyes off herself and focusing on a hurting, needy world.

As we open our eyes to the needs and opportunities for world missions and evangelism, we find ourselves challenged in new ways as we try to obey the words of John's first epistle: "If anyone has material possessions and sees his brother in need but has no pity on him, how can the love of God be in him? Dear children, let us not love with words or tongue but with actions and in truth" (1 John 3:17-18).

Seeing a world of need and endeavoring to respond is both challenging and counter-cultural. We live in an age when we are easily "blinded by pre-occupation with self-fulfillment so that we cannot see the world as God sees it."[1]

Sociologist Daniel Yankelovich reports his findings about our self-centered society in his book, *New Rules:*

Searching for Self-Fulfillment in a World Turned Upside Down. He observes that, by our culture's standard, "The norm is one's duty to one's self . . . to break that norm in such a society . . . is to do wrong."[2] Yankelovich goes on to observe that such self-centeredness is actually destructive to the individual in society:

> By concentrating day and night on your feelings, potentials, needs, wants and desires, and by learning to assert them more freely, you do not become a freer, more spontaneous, more creative self; you become a narrower, more self-centered, more isolated one. You do not grow, you shrink.[3]

None of us want to shrink—either as persons or as Christians who seek to see the world as God sees it. If we choose to grow, however, we have to make personal choices regarding lifestyle, values, and priorities that contradict those of our society.

Our decision to grow in our personal vision for God's world will be positively influenced by our lifestyle choices. We cannot learn about billions of hungry, poor, or malnourished people and remain unchanged if God's love is in us. In a variety of ways, we will be forced to respond by limiting ourselves so we can identify with those in need. St. Francis de Sales presented this message in his book, *Introduction to the Devout Life*:

> If you love the poor you will share their poverty and be poor like them. If you love the poor be often with them. Be glad to see them in your own home and to visit with them in theirs. Be glad to talk to them and be pleased to have them near you in church, on the street, and elsewhere. Be poor when conversing with

them and speak to them as their companions do, but be rich in assisting them by sharing some of your more abundant goods with them.[4]

The simplification of our lifestyle is one way we can choose to identify with those who are less fortunate than we are. Simplification may enable us to give more of our resources, or we may simply be able to share in the sufferings of others in a small way. This is the idea Francis de Sales is trying to communicate, but the idea comes ultimately from our Lord Himself:

> For you know the grace of our Lord Jesus Christ, that though he was rich, yet for your sakes he became poor, so that you through his poverty might become rich. (2 Corinthians 8:9)

Jesus emptied Himself and became a man (Philippians 2:5ff) so that we might be saved. In the same way, those involved in missions (both the sent and the senders) should be willing to sacrifice for the salvation of others. Elisabeth Elliot reiterates this point: "From St. Paul to St. Nicholas of Japan there has been no missions without self-identification of the missionary with those to whom God has sent him, without a sacrifice of his personal attachments and his natural values."[5]

Does this mean we are all called to a life of total renunciation of possessions if we desire to biblically fulfill our obligation toward missions? Not necessarily. A few of us may be called to total renunciation of possessions, but this usually does little overall good for the local or worldwide witness. All of us, however, are called to be stewards, and this is perhaps much more challenging. Total renunciation yields total poverty, which removes our choices. Stewardship, on the other hand, means making wise choices on how to use that which God has entrusted to us.

VOLUNTARY LIMITATION: A BASIC CHOICE

Making the choice to place limits on ourselves is contrary to our culture where one beer commercial exhorts us to "grab for all the gusto," and another asks the rhetorical question, "Who says you can't have it all?" Nevertheless, limitation is the right choice for Christians who are concerned for God's world.

In the book, *Living More Simply*, Howard Claassen offers four goals for simpler living for all world-concerned Christians:

1. The first is to learn to understand the poor by lessening the large economic gap between us and them. The vast majority of the world are very poor. God loves the poor and frequently states his special concern for them in the Bible.

2. A second goal is to try to avoid materialism, the love of possessions and money. That one is tricky. To live frugally and place a large fraction of our income into savings will not do. That savings account may feed our materialism rather than starve it.

3. A third goal is to reduce consumption of resources that are scarce and non-renewable and to reduce pollution of the environment. That involves conservation and the recycling of our waste materials.

4. A fourth goal is to reduce causes of international tensions and wars. Does our country possess the world's strongest military force because we are concerned about protecting the rights of poor and oppressed people or because we feel the need to pro-

tect our freedom to buy resources cheaply in all parts of the world? Probably the second answer is the correct one, and I should, at least, reduce my own contribution to our country's pattern of consumption of resources.[6]

Mr. Claassen goes on to describe the lifestyle choices he and his family have made to simplify their consumption. These choices include driving a ten-year-old car (rather than the new one they could afford), commuting to work on a bicycle (seven miles round trip), and a decision to "give away the portion of income that was above our needs."[7] The Claassens have simplified their life to the point that they are giving fifty percent of their income away (note: their home is paid for).

We may not be able to live as simply as the Claassens, but we can choose to simplify some areas of our lives. Our choices come from the virtue of humility, as exemplified in Christ, which is necessary for those of us who desire Christlikeness. Humility is ultimately "staying close to the ground (*humus*), to people, to everyday life, to what is happening with all its down-to-earthness."[8]

We live in what has been called a "global village," and we need to see ourselves as the wealthier neighbors of the community. Our choices directly affect others, but the fact that we even have the choice reflects our affluence. Perhaps ninety percent of the world lives in a state of poverty where there are few, if any, lifestyle choices.

Perhaps our starting point in simplification is reading. Books like *Living More Simply, Rich Christians in an Age of Hunger, The Golden Cow,* and *The Problem of Wineskins* all offer challenging thoughts on how to simplify our lives, spending, and consumption so that poorer members of our world can benefit.

LIFESTYLE CHOICES WE CAN MAKE AS WORLD CHRISTIANS

Each of us faces our own choices on how we live, how much we give away, and what changes we make to increase our sensitivity to world needs. There are a few categories, however, in which all of us can consider altering our lifestyles or behaviors.

1. Language. With a view toward the world, we will find it difficult, if not impossible, to refer to our own needs as "great." We all have needs, but our world view should help us keep them in proper perspective. When we awaken in the morning, we may want to reconsider our use of the term "hungry" in reference to ourselves. In reality, we may not feel full, but few of us are ever truly hungry. We should certainly eliminate the term "starved" from any references to ourselves.

Our language should also change with respect to unfounded generalizations such as the statement, "People are poor because they do not work hard." Plenty of poor people, in this country and around the world, work very hard, but live in economic systems that do not allow advancement. Even in our own country, according to Dr. Tony Campolo, "The poor often find themselves the victims of social injustice and psychological oppression by a society that equates their poverty with God's disfavor."[9]

2. Money. Rather than focusing on our money as a way to benefit ourselves, we can choose to view our money as a way to benefit others. With this in mind, we can live according to Jesus' example; He gave all that He had for us.

3. Success. One primary reason we become self-centered and strive for personal gain is because we want to be successful in a society that determines success by wealth and possessions. Such a definition of success denies the Bible's teaching regarding Heaven. When we allow wealth and possessions to become the determinants of success, we are assuming that this life is all there is.

From a biblical perspective, we should desire success, but we should desire it from God's perspective. The Bible teaches that we are here on earth in preparation for Heaven. There is a Judgment Day. We will be called into account before God for how we have spent our lives here on earth. Life on earth, however, is not simply a preparation time for life in Heaven. God defines success in His terms in Micah 6:8 (see also Deuteronomy 10:12):

He has showed you, O man what is good.
And what does the LORD require of you?
To act justly and to love mercy
and to walk humbly with your God.

4. Separation. More traditional Christians still refer to the term "separation" when referring to someone's Christian maturity. Basically, the term means the degree to which one keeps separate from the evils of this world—whether those evils be card playing, drinking alcohol, or dancing.

If we are going to choose lifestyles that honor God in light of the world in which we live, we, too, must consider separation. Simplifying our lifestyles is a counter-cultural choice, but we should also note that the advertising world and media can seduce us if we are not concentrating on some aspect of Christian separateness. For example, one commercial tells women to buy a perfume because, "You're worth it." Other advertisements tell me that a Volvo, a Mercedes, or a BMW will guarantee my success and prestige. The American Express Gold Card seeks to assure me that I will be noticed as a person of distinction.

To combat these subtle, and not-so-subtle pleas for self-centeredness, I must see myself as separated from this world's values. Prestige or distinction is not my concern. Instead, my concern is to be a servant under the Master who has called me to accomplish His will in the world. With this as my top priority, I must separate myself from the sinful lures of the world I live in.

5. Simplicity. How does one achieve simplicity in a world where we are told that we will be illiterate in the next ten years if we don't have a computer, and all our friends are buying time-sharing condos, VCRs, and subscribing to cable television?

Simplicity may be as much an attitude as an outward style of living. The simplest person is one who has one goal—to please Jesus Christ in everything. As one of the contributors to the book, *Living More Simply,* says,

> Lost people include those who are poor and those who are rich and those who are in middle-class America. Our hospitals, nursing homes, retirement centers, jails, juvenile homes and shelters for runaways and battered wives—all are full of desperately hurting people. Some people don't need to move; they need to open their eyes, unclutter their lives, empty their closets and open their homes for Jesus' sake and share his goodness and love. The need to communicate the gospel is not limited to any geographic location. Only our vision is limited.[10]

Simplicity is "doing the will of God with a smile," according to Mother Theresa.[11] Our vision can be cluttered by too many things; we need to choose simplicity so we can keep the main focus of missions—the declaration that Jesus Christ is Savior and Lord—as the focus of our lives.

6. Affluence. We need to change our dreams if we are to live lifestyles that are consistent with and complementary to our world vision. We may sing, "Riches I heed not,"[12] but is it true? Many of us enjoy postponing God's call on our possessions and money. We say, "Well, as soon as I make more money, then I will start being generous," or "After we buy our house, then we'll start giving more away."

In reality, we are subtly conditioning ourselves to pursue greater affluence. We want to have, or earn, something beyond what we have now. But after we achieve the first goal, we will make another, higher goal for ourselves until God is—for all practical purposes—pushed out of our lives.

A quotation attributed to Vance Havner addresses the dangers of affluence and success: "As long as the church wore scars, they made headway. When they began to wear medals, the cause languished. It was a greater day for the church when Christians were fed to the lions than when they bought season tickets and sat in the grandstand."

Many of us are financially in the grandstand, but we can still choose to leave the delusion of affluence that has hypnotized our culture. If we do, we will be able to increase our sense of world vision. In a sense, we will be choosing to come out of the grandstand and onto the ground level where most of the world lives.

LIFESTYLE CHOICES: SOME QUESTIONS TO CONSIDER

David Bryant, missions expert for InterVarsity Christian Fellowship, poses some excellent questions to consider as we evaluate our lifestyles according to world Christian priorities These convicting questions will help us grow in our efforts to live lives that are in keeping with our vision for the world:

- What most determines my sense of "needs"? TV? Career? Status? Peers? Or, Christ's global cause and the needs of unreached people?
- Is my lifestyle shaped by a desire for more—more

possessions, more happiness, more power? Or, is it shaped by a desire for increased personal freedom and availability of resources in order to serve the world's unreached?

• What are the excesses in my life? What do I have too much of right now? Where do I presently squander, waste, or overindulge? How will this affect further outreach to the ends of the earth?

• Should my involvement in the cause right now be from surplus or from sacrifice? How might future involvement in the cause be affected by my approach to this?

• Out of my 168 hours a week, can I justify the overall allotment of my time in light of Christ's global cause? What specific time commitments need to be cut back in order to prepare me for increased future outreach? Are there places my investments of time should be rechanneled right now?

• Of the decisions I am making right now which ones will have a lasting impact on how involved I am in the worldwide outreach in the future? Which decisions might increase my effectiveness over what it is now? How should love for the unreached guide my choices, such as where to live, whom to marry, what profession to pursue, new friendships to seek, purchases, prayer and Bible reading habits, service on a church committee, family size, magazine subscriptions, or Christian conferences I attend?[13]

A CONVICTING STORY IN ETHIOPIA

A friend of mine is a television newscaster. In the midst of the publicity surrounding the famine in northern Africa, he was sent to Ethiopia to do a special report. After his trip, we discussed his experiences. The horrible memories of seeing children die and mothers wail left deep impressions on my friend, but one of the deepest scars was made in a conversation he had with a political leader. The Ethiopian leader asked my friend, "Why are you here? Why not just let them all die?" My friend was horrified at the man's callousness.

I listened with disbelief to that story, but as I thought about it, I realized that I could become as calloused as that Ethiopian leader. If my lifestyle, personal spending, and use of resources go unchanged after hearing such stories, I am, in effect, saying the same thing: "Why not just let them all die?"

I may not be able to help the people in Ethiopia directly, but I must be willing to modify my lifestyle so I can be a more responsible steward of what God has given me to manage in His world. I must be willing to love with action and in truth.

NOTES:

1. J. Robertson McQuilkin, *The Great Omission* (Grand Rapids: Baker Book House, 1984), page 25.
2. Daniel Yankelovich, *New Rules: Searching for Self-Fulfillment in a World Turned Upside Down* (New York: Random House, 1981), page 175.
3. Yankelovich, page 242.
4. Quoted in *Discipleship Journal* (Issue #25, 1985), page 33.
5. Elisabeth Elliot, *Discipline: The Glad Surrender* (New York: Harper and Row, 1982), page 142.
6. Howard Claassen, "Struggling Free in the Family: Guidelines and Models," Ronald Sider, ed., *Living More Simply* (Downers Grove, Illinois: InterVarsity Press, 1980), pages 96-97.
7. Claassen.
8. Henri Nouwen, *¡Gracias! A Latin American Journal* (New York: Harper and Row, 1983), page 162.
9. Anthony Campolo, Jr., *The Success Fantasy* (Wheaton, Illinois: Victor Books, 1980), page 142.
10. *Living More Simply*, page 171.
11. Malcolm Muggeridge, *Something Beautiful for God* (New York: Harper and Row, 1971), page 67.
12. Verse 4 of the hymn "Be Thou My Vision," *Hymns II* (Downers Grove, Illinois: InterVarsity Press, 1976), page 18.
13. David Bryant, *In the Gap* (Downers Grove, Illinois: InterVarsity Press, 1977), pages 228-229.

Other Input

In Deuteronomy 30:19-20, Moses set a choice before the people of Israel: Life versus death, blessings versus curses. He urged them to choose life, and listen to God's voice, and "hold fast to him." We need to make the same choices every day—obediently loving God, and holding fast to Him.

Living the Christian life involves making many daily and lifetime choices. Will we adhere to a selfish brand of Christianity that sees God as the heavenly giver of health and wealth? Will we become preoccupied with nit-picking Christianity—which is side-tracked by peripheral doctrines that separate Christians rather than uniting us together for the worldwide task before us?

God gives us many choices. If we are to stay close to God and share His vision for the world, we must be willing to make choices that will help us to go out of our way to keep the goal of world missions and evangelization on our hearts. This chapter concentrates on the casual, yet purposeful, choices we can make to build and increase our love for and commitment to the world.

In the same way as we are commanded to keep God's Word always in front of us (Deuteronomy 6:6-7, 11:18-20), we can also choose to keep the world before us. Dawson Trotman, the visionary founder of The Navigators, describes what happened when they started setting the world before them:

> We sure didn't start out praying big, but we ended up praying, "Lord, allow us to serve you in every continent of the world." We didn't know all that we were asking for, but God did, and that's all that counts. Things began to change when one of us . . . remarked to the other, "Let's get a map of the world."[1]

Setting the world before them by looking at a map helped the early Navigator leaders gain a vision for the world.

The Navigator director of the campus where I went to college—the University of Massachusetts—enjoyed telling the story of Waldron Scott, one of the early Navigators who worked in South America. (Scott went on to become director of World Evangelical Fellowship, and later served as leader of the American Leprosy Mission.) The world vision that characterized "Scotty" was formed in his childhood. Evidently, Scotty had a lung problem as a child. To help him build his lung power, he would blow up balloons. The balloons had maps of the world on them, and it was this daily exposure that started young Waldron Scott thinking about the world.

SETTING THE WORLD BEFORE US

David exemplifies one who set his heart on God's Word. Psalm 119 is the testimony of a man who chose to concentrate on God's Word: "I have chosen the way of truth," the psalmist writes in verse 30. "I have set my heart on your laws."

As we saw in building block one, setting our hearts on God's laws can show us His concern and plan for the world. Therefore, setting our hearts on His laws can lead us to set our hearts on His purposes for the world. But how? Obviously, the building block suggestions of this book are designed to help us keep a world vision before us, but there are other entertaining and educational avenues we can pursue to keep our eyes and minds focused beyond ourselves.

1. Make the world our hobby. Should something as serious as world missions be called a hobby? No, not if we think of missions only when we have free time or only on our vacations. But making education about the world our hobby can greatly facilitate our overall commitment to missions. If we are always looking for opportunities to learn more about the world, it will help us grow as world Christians.

This is why, after reading the news, I turn to the "Travel" section of the Sunday newspaper. Although I do not look at the places advertised as a potential tourist, I always seek to learn more about new places. I go into travel agencies to look at their most exotic brochures, because many of these exotic places—Lhasa, Tibet, or Papua New Guinea—are also frontiers of missions.

I make world learning my hobby. My wife and I pursue this together, and we subscribe to travel magazines and *National Geographic* just to learn more about the world. We see movies like "Out of Africa" or "Passage to India" to learn more about our world. We go out of our way to watch programs on educational television about the world's people and cultures.

2. Keep the world visible. Over the years, my wife and I have dedicated ourselves to learning about the world's geography. As a result, we buy "trinkets" that have a world map on them. For example, we now own

- a desk blotter with a world map on it
- several wall maps of the world
- earrings with miniature globes on them
- coffee mugs with world maps on them

- a world globe beach ball
- a world globe pencil sharpener
- a world globe paperweight.

Several of our friends have caught a similar vision. One friend purchased a world globe necklace, but we were outdone by our friends Rod and Jan. In a conversation with them about an international student from Mauritius who was coming to our church, they told us they did not know where that country was, but they promised to "check the shower curtain when they got home."

"What does the shower curtain have to do with Mauritius?" I inquired.

"We have a shower curtain with a map of the world on it," they replied.

Setting the world before us: it can be a fun way to remember that we are only in one small geographic point in God's world plan.

3. Learn about the places of the world. Our reading and world maps help us keep the world in front of us, but we do not learn much unless we supplement the visual stimuli with intellectual stimuli. To do this, we also need to pursue active learning. Here are a few suggestions that can add to our world knowledge.

Become an expert on the blue section of the "Trivial Pursuit" game. These geographical questions can help us learn about the world and its people.

Look for other geographical or world-focused educational games. A game like "Where in the World"[2] is distinctly educational and can provide us with great information to supplement our missions praying and learning.

Make up games to make missions learning fun. This can be done by using an up-to-date atlas or encyclopedia. One example might be a family game where the person with a resource book names a country, and the participants are scored on the basis of what they know: one point if they can identify the correct continent, another if they can find it on a map, a third if they can name the capital city, and a fourth if they can identify the main language spoken there.

Another game that can be played in a family setting is what I call "missions roulette." A globe on a spinning axis is needed to play this game. The person with the globe spins it and another family member (either blindfolded or looking away) points to a particular spot. The person who chose the spot pretends to be a missionary to that location. He or she tells about the language, clothing, topography, and climate and is scored accordingly. (*Note:* Make it plain that when a spot selected is in the ocean, the closest island or country is chosen. This is necessary because there is a two-out-of-three chance to point to water.)

A variation on missions roulette is to work in teams. Provide basic missions resource guides or encyclopedias so that information is available about the places to which each team points. Then, after the teams do some research, they can present a brief skit on how a missionary might look or act in that country.

4. Start young. These games and activities are good for adult missions education, but they are also a tremendous way of exposing young children to missions. Missions education and a love for God's world can be instilled in children at a young age if these activities are pursued and supplemented with visits from missionaries, prayer for missions, and Bible memorization.

The leaders of Overseas Crusades addressed this matter in their *Lost and Found* newsletter:

A Christian home without missions is tragically inadequate. How can we disregard the importance of one of Christ's final commands to all believers—the Great Commission—in our families' goals and decisions? If we have left the job of missions education to the church, the mission agency, or the Christian school, we have missed the very place to start. Missions begins in the home. Any other influence is trivial in comparison. Missionary interests, prejudices, stereotypes—one's entire outlook on world evangelization—is developed largely within the home. This 24-hour-a-day missions learning environment is unmatched by any other educational setting.[3]

Keeping the world in front of every family member is a great way to keep enthusiasm and commitment high when considering what your involvement as a family can be in world vision and missions.[4]

OTHER INPUT—BECAUSE MISSIONS IS A PRIORITY

Why do we go to the expense of buying the world globe trinkets with which we decorate our home? Why do some of my friends listen to international radio (like HCJB in Ecuador, or Trans World Radio)? Why would someone buy a world map shower curtain or an expensive, global educational game?

The reason is this: God has called us into this world to be His lights and witnesses, and we choose to make His world a focus of our attention. His global concerns are our priorities, and we surround ourselves with reminders of His world perspective.

So, the next time you see a world map beach ball, the next time an international program is on television, or the next time a question in the blue section of "Trivial Pursuit" comes up, don't just ignore it! God could use it to help you develop your world vision!

NOTES:
1. Robert D. Foster, *The Navigator* (Colorado Springs, Colorado: NavPress, 1983), page 191.
2. "Where in the World—A World Awareness Game" for ages eight and up is produced by Aristoplay, Ltd., P.O. Box 7645, Ann Arbor, Michigan 48107.
3. From Overseas Crusades' newsletter *Lost and Found* (Fall 1982).
4. The Association of Church Missions Committees (P.O. Box ACMC, Wheaton, Illinois 60189) publishes a variety of missions education material including the *Missions Education Handbook* which, although it is written for use in the church or Sunday school, has some ideas and games that can be used at home.

Conclusion

We began our study with a choice—to become *worldly Christians* or *world Christians*. The fact that you have read this book indicates that you desire to be a world Christian, but becoming a world Christian is an ongoing process that requires us to continue making choices toward that end for the rest of our lives.

The challenge of world missions and the requirements of developing our world vision can cause us to overreact. Sam Wilson and Gordon Aeschliman point out the extreme responses to missions in their book, *The Hidden Half*: "You can get overwhelmed and hide under your bed or escape to the mountains. Or you can forget you're human and try to go without food or sleep. But neither response will have a lasting impact on the needy of the world."[1]

The far better choice is to start building a vision for God's world. Use the building blocks of prayer, firsthand cross-cultural experience, learning from Scripture, current events, missions resources, and other guidelines suggested in this book. Then respond to the Lord as He directs, and He will help us take our eyes off ourselves, increase our burden for the lost, intensify our prayers, and gain a greater sense of where He wants to use us in His master plan.

WILL WE PULL DOWN THE BLINDS?

Tony Campolo describes an experience he had in the very poor country of Haiti:

> During a visit to Haiti, I went to a restaurant. The waiter seated me by a large window. He took my order and then brought me a very attractive dinner. I was about to eat a bite of steak when I happened to look to my left. Eight hungry Haitian children, with their noses pressed up against the glass, were staring at my food. I immediately lost my appetite and set the fork down. The waiter, seeing what was happening, quickly moved in and pulled down the venetian blind. He said to me, "Enjoy your meal. Don't let them bother you."[2]

As we begin to understand the biblical and practical ways God wants us to be involved in a needy world, we may be upset by the inequities and injustices we see. The thought of three billion people who have no knowledge of the Savior Jesus Christ, or the realization that we are "rich Christians in an age of hunger,"[3] can cause us to want to "pull down the blinds" so we can enjoy our lives without being bothered by those who are beyond our immediate reach.

But as world Christians, we must leave the blinds open, and, in full view of the world into which God has called us, decide how and where to be part of the solution.

GIVE UP SMALL AMBITIONS

Michael Griffiths of Overseas Missionary Fellowship wrote a missions book titled, *Give Up Your Small Ambitions.* The title was taken from the exhortation of Francis Xavier, the sixteenth-century Jesuit missionary to India, China, and Japan.

Xavier is said to have longed to go back to Paris, "shouting up and down the streets to tell the students to give up their small ambitions and come eastward to preach the gospel of Christ."[4] What are our ambitions? Are they small? Are they worldly Christian ambitions that seek comfort and ease? Are we looking for a self-centered relationship with God that will bring personal happiness and self-fulfillment? Or do we have great ambitions? Do we desire to be world Christians whose entire lives are turned around because Jesus Christ is our first love? Are we people who look beyond ourselves, letting God determine the outcome of our lives as we seek to obey Him in His call to the world? Are we willing to give whatever our Lord asks of us?

Jim Elliot and his four partners in ministry gave up their small ambitions to serve the Lord and, in obedience to Him, served the Auca Indians of Ecuador. With great ambitions of serving Him, they marched out to meet those Indians. As they went, they sang the great sending hymn:

"We rest on Thee"—our Shield and our Defender!
We go not forth alone against the foe;
Strong in Thy strength, safe in Thy keeping tender,
"We rest on Thee, and in Thy name we go."[5]

With our great ambition to be pleasing to God (see 2 Corinthians 5:9) we, too, can build toward the goal of being committed world Christians—going forth in His strength! Let's build!

NOTES:
1. Sam Wilson and Gordon Aeschliman, *The Hidden Half* (Monrovia, California: MARC, n.d.), page 22.
2. Anthony Campolo, Jr., *The Success Fantasy* (Wheaton, Illinois: Victor Books,

1980), page 144.

3. This is the title of one of Ronald Sider's books (Downers Grove, Illinois: Inter-Varsity Press, 1977).

4. Michael Griffiths, *Give Up Your Small Ambitions* (Chicago: Moody Press, 1970), page 6.

5. From *Hymns II* (Downers Grove, Illinois: InterVarsity Press, 1976), page 170.

Further Reading

HISTORIES AND BIOGRAPHIES

Adeney, David H. *China: Christian Students Face the Revolution.* Downers Grove, Illinois: InterVarsity Press, 1973.

Adeney, David H. *China: The Church's Long March.* Ventura, California: Regal Books, 1985.

Bacon, Daniel W. *From Faith to Faith.* Robesonia, Pennsylvania: OMF Books, 1984.

Bailey, Faith Coxe, ed. *Adoniram Judson: America's First Foreign Missionary.* Chicago, Illinois: Moody Press, 1955.

Bentley-Taylor, David. *My Love Must Wait.* Downers Grove, Illinois: InterVarsity Press, 1975.

Boardman, Robert. *A Higher Honor.* Colorado Springs, Colorado: NavPress, 1986.

Brainerd, David. *The Life and Diary of David Brainerd.* Newark, Delaware: Cornerstone, n.d.

Buchan, James. *The Expendable Mary Slessor.* New York: Seabury Press, 1981.

Dekker, John. *Torches of Joy.* Westchester, Illinois: Crossway Books, 1985.

Deyneka, Anita and Peter. *Christians in the Shadow of the*

Kremlin. Elgin, Illinois: David C. Cook Publishing Company, 1974.

Dunker, Marilee Pierce. *Man of Vision, Woman of Prayer.* Nashville, Tennessee: Thomas Nelson Publishers, 1980.

Elliot, Elisabeth. *The Shadow of the Almighty.* Grand Rapids, Michigan: Zondervan Publishing House, 1958.

Elliot, Elisabeth. *Through Gates of Splendor.* Wheaton, Illinois: Living Books, 1981.

Elliot, Elisabeth. *Who Shall Ascend?* New York: Harper and Row, 1968.

Estes, Steve. *Called to Die.* Grand Rapids: Zondervan Publishing House, 1986.

Foster, Robert D. *The Navigator.* Colorado Springs: NavPress, 1983.

Freed, Paul E. *Towers to Eternity.* Nashville: Thomas Nelson Publishers, 1979.

Fuller, Millard. *No More Shacks!* Waco, Texas: Word, Inc., 1986.

Goforth, Rosalind. *Jonathan Goforth.* Minneapolis, Minnesota: Bethany House Publishers, 1986.

Graham, Franklin. *Bob Pierce: This One Thing I Do.* Waco, Texas: Word, Inc., 1983.

Green, Julian. *God's Fool.* New York: Harper and Row, 1985.

Grubb, Norman P. *C.T. Studd: Cricketer and Pioneer.* Fort Washington, Pennsylvania: Christian Literature Crusade, 1979.

Hall, Clarence W. *Miracle on the Sepik.* Costa Mesa, California: Gift Publications, 1980.

Hefley, James and Marti. *Uncle Cam.* Waco, Texas: Word, Inc., 1974.

Howard, David M. *The Dream That Would Not Die.* Exeter, England: Paternoster Press, 1986.

Howard, David M. *Hammered as Gold.* London: Lakeland, 1969.

Howard, David M. *Student Power in World Evangelism.* Downers Grove, Illinois: InterVarsity Press, 1970.

Jay, Ruth Johnson. *Mary Slessor: White Queen of the Cannibals.* Chicago: Moody Press, 1985.

Lapping, Brian. *End of Empire.* New York: St. Martin's Press, 1985.

Larson, Robert C. *Wansui: Insights on China Today.* Waco, Texas: Word, Inc., 1974.

Lawrence, Carl. *The Church in China.* Minneapolis: Bethany House Publishers, 1985.

Lutz, Lorry. *Destined for Royalty.* Pasadena, California: William Carey Library, 1985.

Lyall, Lesley T. *New Spring in China.* Grand Rapids: Zondervan Publishing House, 1980.

Miller, Basil. *George Mueller: Man of Faith and Miracles.* Minneapolis: Bethany House Publishers, 1941.

Miller, Basil. *William Carey.* Minneapolis: Bethany House Publishers, 1980.

Morrow, Honore Willsie. *Splendor of God.* Grand Rapids: Baker Book House, 1929.

Muggeridge, Malcom. *Something Beautiful for God.* New York: Harper and Row, 1971.

Olson, Bruce E. *Bruchko.* Carol Stream, Illinois: Creation House, 1978.

OMF. *When God Guides.* Robesonia, Pennsylvania: OMF Books, 1984.

OMF. *When the Roof Caves In.* Robesonia, Pennsylvania: OMF Books, 1985.

Paulson, Hank. *Beyond the Wall.* Ventura, California: Regal Books, 1982.

Perkins, John. *Let Justice Roll Down.* Ventura, California: Regal Books, 1976.

Pollock, J.C. *Hudson Taylor and Maria.* Grand Rapids: Zondervan Publishing House, 1962.

Popov, Haralan. *Tortured for His Faith*. Grand Rapids: Zondervan Publishing House, 1970.

Richardson, Don. *Eternity in Their Hearts*. Ventura, California: Regal Books, 1981.

Richardson, Don. *Lords of the Earth*. Ventura, California: Regal Books, 1976.

Richardson, Don. *Peace Child*. Ventura, California: Regal Books, 1974.

Roseveare, Helen. *He Gave Us a Valley*. Downers Grove, Illinois: InterVarsity Press, 1976.

Sanders, J. Oswald. *Just Like Us*. Chicago: Moody Press, 1978.

Stanffacher, Gladys. *Faster Beats the Drum*. Pearl River, New York: Africa Inland Mission, 1977.

Steven, Hugh. *Good Broth to Warm Our Bones*. Westchester, Illinois: Crossway Books, 1982.

Steven, Hugh. *Never Touch a Tiger*. Nashville: Thomas Nelson Publishers, 1980.

Student Missions Power. Pasadena, California: William Carey Library, n.d.

Taylor, Dr. and Mrs. Howard. *Hudson Taylor's Spiritual Secret*. Philadelphia, Pennsylvania: China Inland Mission, 1958.

Taylor, J. Hudson. *To China . . . With Love*. Minneapolis: Bethany House Publishers, 1972.

Tucker, Ruth A. *From Jerusalem to Irian Jaya*. Grand Rapids: Zondervan Publishing House, 1983.

Wiersbe, Warren W. *Victorious Christians You Should Know*. Grand Rapids: Baker Book House, 1984.

Winebrenner, Jan. *Steel in His Soul: The Dick Hillis Story*. San Jose, California: OC Ministries, 1985.

Worcester, J.H., Jr. *The Life of David Livingstone*. Chicago: Moody Press, 1888.

Wurmbrand, Richard. *Tortured for Christ*. Glendale, California: Diane Books, 1969.

ISSUES IN MISSIONS TODAY

Aeschliman, Gordon D. *Apartheid: Tragedy in Black and White*. Ventura, California: Regal Books, 1986.

Barrett, David B. *World-Class Cities and World Evangelization*. Birmingham, Alabama: New Hope, 1986.

Beals, Paul A. *A People for His Name*. Pasadena, California: William Carey Library, 1985.

Clouse, Robert G., ed. *Wealth and Poverty*. Downers Grove, Illinois: InterVarsity Press, 1984.

Cosmao, Vincent. *Changing the World: An Agenda for the Churches*. Maryknoll, New York: Orbis Books, 1984.

Dayton, Edward R. and David A. Fraser. *Planning Strategies for World Evangelization*. Grand Rapids, Michigan: Wm. B. Eerdmans Publishing Company, 1980.

Douglas, Donald E., ed. *Evangelical Perspectives on China*. Farmington, Michigan: Evangelical China Committee, 1976.

Engstrom, Ted W. *What in the World Is God Doing?* Waco, Texas: Word, Inc., 1978.

Glasser, Arthur F. and Donald A. McGavran. *Contemporary Theologies of Mission*. Grand Rapids: Baker Book House, 1983.

Howard, David M. *The Great Commission for Today*. Downers Grove, Illinois: InterVarsity Press, 1976.

Johnston, Arthur. *The Battle for World Evangelism*. Wheaton, Illinois: Tyndale House Publishers, 1978.

Kane, J. Herbert. *Winds of Change in the Christian Mission*. Chicago, Illinois: Moody Press, 1973.

Kyle, John E., ed. *The Unfinished Task*. Ventura, California: Regal Books, 1984.

Lau, Lawson. *The World at Your Doorstep*. Downers Grove, Illinois: InterVarsity Press, 1984.

McGavran, Donald, ed. *Eye of the Storm*. Waco, Texas: Word,

Inc., 1972.

Mooneyham, Stan. *Is There Life Before Death?* Ventura, California: Regal Books, 1985.

Mulholland, Kenneth B. *Adventures in Training the Ministry.* Nutley, New Jersey: Presbyterian and Reformed, 1976.

Murray, Andrew. *The State of the Church.* Kempton Park, South Africa: The Andrew Murray Consultation on Prayer for Revival and Missions, 1985.

Nouwen, Henri J.M. *¡Gracias! A Latin American Journal.* New York: Harper and Row, 1983.

Nunez, Emilio A. *Liberation Theology.* Chicago: Moody Press, 1985.

Peace, Judy Boppell. *The Boy Child Is Dying.* Downers Grove, Illinois: InterVarsity Press, 1978.

Roberts, W. Dayton, ed. *Africa: A Season For Hope.* Ventura, California: Regal Books, 1985.

Salley, Columbus and Ronald Behm. *What Color Is Your God?* Downers Grove, Illinois: InterVarsity Press, 1981.

Schell, Orville. *In the People's Republic.* New York: Random House, 1977.

Sider, Ronald J., ed. *Living More Simply.* Downers Grove, Illinois: InterVarsity Press, 1980.

Sider, Ronald J. *Rich Christians in an Age of Hunger.* Downers Grove, Illinois: InterVarsity Press, 1977.

Stott, John R.W. *Christian Mission in the Modern World.* Downers Grove, Illinois: InterVarsity Press, 1977.

Unger, Merrill F. *Demons in the World Today.* Wheaton: Tyndale House Publishers, 1971.

Wagner, C. Peter. *Frontiers in Missionary Strategy.* Chicago: Moody Press, 1971.

Wagner, C. Peter. *On the Crest of the Wave.* Ventura, California: Regal Books, 1983.

Wilson, J. Christy, Jr. *Afghanistan: The Forbidden Harvest.* Elgin, Illinois: David C. Cook Publishing Co., 1981.

Wilson, J. Christy, Jr. *Today's Tentmakers*. Wheaton: Tyndale House Publishers, 1979.

Yohannan, K.P. *The Coming Revolution in World Missions*. Altamonte Springs, Florida: Creation House, 1986.

Zionels, David. *A Christian View of Russia*. South Plainfield, New Jersey: Bridge Publishing, 1983.

UNDERSTANDING CROSS-CULTURAL WORK

Bavinck, J.H. *An Introduction to the Science of Missions*. Philipsburg, New Jersey: Presbyterian and Reformed, 1979.

Collins, Marjorie A. *Manual for Today's Missionary*. Pasadena, California: William Carey Library, 1986.

Eims, LeRoy. *Laboring in the Harvest*. Colorado Springs, Colorado: NavPress, 1985.

Elliot, Elisabeth. *No Graven Image*. New York: Harper and Row, 1966.

Finley, Allen and Lorry Lutz. *Mission: A World Family Affair*. San Jose, California: Christian National Press, 1981.

Foster, George M. *Traditional Societies and Technological Change*. New York: Harper and Row, 1973.

Gallagher, Neil. *Don't Go Overseas Until You've Read This Book*. Minneapolis: Bethany House Publishers, 1977.

Griffiths, Michael C. *Give Up Your Small Ambitions*. Chicago: Moody Press, 1970.

Hillis, Don W. *I Don't Feel Called (Thank the Lord!)* Wheaton, Illinois: Tyndale House Publishers, 1973.

Kane, J. Herbert. *Life and Work on the Mission Field*. Grand Rapids, Michigan: Baker Book House, 1980.

Kane, J. Herbert. *The Making of a Missionary*. Grand Rapids, Michigan: Baker Book House, 1975.

Kohls, L. Robert. *Survival Kit for Overseas Living*. Yarmouth, Maine: Intercultural Press, 1984.

Lockerbie, Jeannie. *By One's and By Two's.* Pasadena, California: William Carey Library, 1983.

Luzbetak, Louis J. *The Church and Cultures.* Pasadena, California: William Carey Library, 1970.

Marsh, C.R. *Share Your Faith with a Muslim.* Chicago, Illinois: Moody Press, 1975.

Mayers, Marvin K. *Christianity Confronts Culture.* Grand Rapids: Zondervan Publishing House, 1974.

Nida, Eugene A. *Customs and Cultures.* Pasadena, California: William Carey Library, 1954.

Parshall, Phil. *Bridges to Islam.* Grand Rapids: Baker Book House, 1983.

Stafford, Tim. *The Friendship Gap.* Downers Grove, Illinois: InterVarsity Press, 1984.

Tingle, Donald S. *Islam and Christianity.* Downers Grove, Illinois: InterVarsity Press, 1985.

Troutman, Charles. *Everything You Want to Know About the Mission Field But Are Afraid You Won't Learn Until You Get There.* Downers Grove, Illinois: InterVarsity Press, 1970.

VISION-BUILDING RESOURCES

Adeney, Miriam. *God's Foreign Policy.* Grand Rapids, Michigan: Wm. B. Eerdmans Publishing Company, 1984.

Anderson, Virginia. *Making Missions Meaningful.* Wheaton, Illinois: Pioneer Girls, 1966.

Author Unknown. *The Kneeling Christian.* Grand Rapids: Zondervan Publishing House, 1971.

Barrett, David B., ed. *World Christian Encyclopedia.* New York: Oxford University Press, 1982.

Beals, Paul A. *A People for His Name.* Pasadena, California: William Carey Library, 1985.

Beckwith, Paul, ed. *Hymns II.* Downers Grove, Illinois: Inter-

Varsity Press, 1976.

Bifocals—Bible study series. Association of Church Missions Committees, P.O. Box ACMC, Wheaton, Illinois 60189.

Bounds, E.M. *Power Through Prayer.* Grand Rapids: Baker Book House, 1972.

Bryant, David. *In the Gap.* Downers Grove, Illinois: InterVarsity Press, 1979.

Bryant, David. *With Concerts of Prayer.* Ventura, California: Regal Books, 1984.

Campolo, Anthony, Jr. *The Success Fantasy.* Wheaton: Victor Books, 1980.

Conn, Harvie M., ed. *Reaching the Unreached.* Philipsburg, New Jersey: Presbyterian and Reformed, 1984.

Douglas, J.D., ed. *Let the Earth Hear His Voice.* Minneapolis, Minnesota: World Wide Publications, 1975.

DuBose, Francis M., ed. *Classics of Christian Missions.* Nashville, Tennessee: Broadman Press, 1979.

Dyer, Kevin G. *Increase Your Vision.* Prospect Heights, Illinois: Selective Distributors, Inc., 1986.

Dyrness, William A. *Let the Earth Rejoice!* Westchester, Illinois: Crossway Books, 1983.

Elliot, Elisabeth. *No Graven Image.* New York: Harper and Row, 1966.

Evangelical Missions Information Service, P.O. Box 794, Wheaton, Illinois 60189.

Fenton, Horace L., Jr. *Myths About Missions.* Downers Grove, Illinois: InterVarsity Press, 1973.

Goldsmith, Martin. *Don't Just Stand There!* Downers Grove, Illinois: InterVarsity Press, 1976.

Gordon, A.J. *The Holy Spirit in Missions.* Harrisburg, Pennsylvania: Christian Publications, 1968.

Hardy, Steven A. *The Final Frontier: Exploring God's Plan for World Missions.* Ventura, California: Gospel Light Publications, 1985.

Hay, A.R. *The New Testament Order for Church and Missionary.* Audubon, New Jersey: New Testament Missionary Union, n.d.

Howard, David M. *By the Power of the Holy Spirit.* Downers Grove, Illinois: InterVarsity Press, 1973.

InterVarsity Missions, 233 Langdon, Madison, Wisconsin 53703.

Kane, J. Herbert. *A Global View of Christian Missions.* Grand Rapids: Baker Book House, 1975.

Kane, J. Herbert. *Wanted: World Christians.* Grand Rapids: Baker Book House, 1986.

McCurry, Donald M., ed. *The Gospel and Islam.* Monrovia, California: MARC, 1979.

McQuilken, J. Robertson. *The Great Omission.* Grand Rapids: Baker Book House, 1984.

Miller, Calvin. *Fred 'n' Erma.* Downers Grove, Illinois: InterVarsity Press, 1986.

"Missions Strategy of the Local Church." Monrovia, California: MARC, 1982.

Neill, Stephen et. al., eds. *Concise Dictionary of the Christian World Mission.* Nashville: Abingdon Press, 1971.

Operation Mobilization, P.O. Box 48, Bromley, Kent, England.

Penny, Ines. *Never Hide a Hyena in a Sack.* Scarborough, Ontario: SIM Books, 1984.

Petersen, Jim. *Living Proof.* Colorado Springs, Colorado: NavPress, 1989.

Shedd, Charlie W. *The Exciting Church—Where They Give Their Money Away.* Waco, Texas: Word, Inc., 1975.

Smith, Oswald J. *The Challenge of Missions.* Bromley, England: STL Books, 1959.

U.S. Center for World Mission, 1605 East Elizabeth, Pasadena, California 91104.

Wagner, C. Peter. *Spiritual Power and Church Growth.* Altamonte Springs, Florida: Strong Communications, 1986.

Wells, Tom. *A Vision For Missions.* Carlisle, Pennsylvania: Banner of Truth Trust, 1985.

What Does It Mean to Be a World Christian? Coral Gables, Florida: WORLDTEAM, 1978.

Wilson, Sam and Gordon Aeschliman. *The Hidden Half.* Monrovia, California: MARC, n.d.

Winter, Ralph D. and Steven C. Hawthorne, eds. *Perspectives on the World Christian Movement.* Pasadena, California: William Carey Library, 1981.

World Christian Magazine, P.O. Box 40010, Pasadena, California 91104.